UPWARD

Taking Your Life to the Next Level

-by-

Gregg T. Johnson

Global Leadership Training
2016

ISBN 978-0-9741036-6-2

Special thank you to Janet Spinelli-Dunn for proofreading and editing

Additional copies of this book are available by mail.
Send $10.00 for each copy requested
(includes tax and postage) to:

Global Leadership Training
c/o The Mission Church
4101 Route 52, Holmes NY 12531, USA

www.GreggTJohnson.com

A portion of the proceeds goes to equipping Christian Leaders around the world

Printed in the United States by Morris Publishing®
3212 East Highway 30 • Kearney, NE 68847
1-800-650-7888

“ *Every next level of your life will require a different you. What got you here, won’t get you there.*

TABLE OF CONTENTS

FOREWORD

by Rev. Dr. Stephen Wengam

In this masterpiece of a book, the author impeccably establishes a truth about people in our time: Although they *desire* to go to the next level, they are not willing to make that *climb* to get to that next level. Indeed, this is the generation that wants a crown without a cross. No wonder there are only a few chosen people who excel in every area.

Pastor Gregg hits the nail on the head by intimating that the way to the next level is a struggle. Thus, there is no sudden flight to the top.

Another important truth he emphasizes is that each person's journey is unique. Thus, though other people's examples may inspire you, they may not necessarily be relevant for you. We must, therefore, be discerning of those whose examples we choose to inspire us.

I am glad Pastor Gregg mentions in this book that moving your life to the next level is pursuing excellence in *every* area. He intimates that excellence is never an option: How can one claim to have made significant progress when one is living a mediocre life? He outlines the practical steps one can take to achieve excellence. Critical among these steps is to consistently stretch yourself in reaching toward the upper range of your talents and skills.

Excellence will distinguish you and, thereby, characterize you as a highly sought-after prospect.

Mental toughness is very critical in the journey to the top. Pastor Gregg skillfully recommends that one develops the spirit of persistence, perseverance, endurance, and resilience. Again, he hits the nail on the head when he portrays this excellent exposition on diligence.

For those aspiring to rise on the leadership ladder, I am excited that Pastor Gregg recommends developing people skills and building competence, as effective leadership largely revolves around these two aspects.

Chapter six deals with moral virtue, the most important foundation of every life. The author highlights the importance of character, which is lost to the world today. He cautions readers about the three things that easily destroy aspiring, emerging, and practicing leaders. They are the gold (money), girls (sexual immorality), and the glory (pride).

We must, therefore, excel in character by pursuing integrity and sexual purity. This comes from having a healthy spiritual life, establishing the truth that the quality of one's character is determined by the quality of one's spiritual life.

Pastor Gregg concludes this book on an excellent note by reminding readers that "what got you here, won't get you there." He calls for re-orientation and recalibration. He advises against complacency and failing to deal with the setbacks in your life.

This book is very timely and apt for the season. I have read all of the books authored by Pastor Gregg and, dare I say, this one encompasses all he has ever written, stands for, and wishes for his generation.

He has been described by many influential leaders in Africa as being God-sent, especially because his teachings and writings focus so well on character and integrity.

Having known Pastor Gregg for a little over a decade, I can confidently say that this author walks the talk. He is a living example of the contents of this book. These teachings of his have transformed many lives in Africa through the Global Leadership Training Conferences.

I recommend this book for all who desire to make significant progress in this journey of life.

Rev. Dr. Stephen Wengam
Chairman, Ghana Prisons Service Council
Lead Pastor, Cedar Mountain Chapel

INTRODUCTION

UPWARD

> **“** ***Everything worthwhile in your life is uphill. ...Everything.***
>
> ***- John Maxwell***

Have you ever seen those preachers offering special anointing oils or “Holy Ghost” hankies that supposedly contain supernatural power to make you prosper, receive a miracle or catch a healing?

Recently, while in East Africa I heard about the “anointed broom” with which you can sweep the devil out of your house, and the “prophetic pen” that guarantees an “A-grade” to students who use it on exams. Of course, there’s the ubiquitous “miracle anointing oil” that will heal any sickness, break any curse, release untold riches, and generally invoke God’s blessing on anything it touches. It’s modern day heresy in a clerical collar.

What amazes me more than the heretical gimmickry coming from pulpits is the eager gullibility of those who actually buy into it. It’s indicative of a mentality so prevalent in the human condition today. We want “it” now. It’s the “quick-fix,” “easy-come,” “give-it-to-me-right-away” attitude. We want the devil out of our house, but we don’t want to fast and pray or do spiritual warfare. We want an “A-grade” on the exam, but we don’t want to study, prepare or memorize. We want the miracles, but we don’t want to hear about the responsibilities we have that facilitate such works. It’s like the mountaineer who says he wants to go the next level, but is unwilling to climb. Just lay hands on me and prophesy, just pour oil on me or pray and let God float me upward without any effort being expended on my part.

Sorry. It doesn't work that way. Just ask the mother of James and John. Her encounter with Christ exposes a gross miscalculation that many make when desiring "the next level."

In Matthew 20:20-23, she came to Jesus with her sons, knelt down and asked something from Him.

> *He said to her, "What do you wish?" She said to Him, "Grant that these two sons of mine may sit, one on Your right hand and the other on the left, in Your kingdom." But Jesus answered and said, "You do not know what you ask. Are you able to drink the cup that I am about to drink, and be baptized with the baptism that I am baptized with?" They said to Him, "We are able." So He said to them, "You will indeed drink My cup, and be baptized with the baptism that I am baptized with; but to sit on My right hand and on My left is not Mine to give, but it is for those for whom it is prepared by My Father." (Matthew 20:20-23)*

She wanted her boys to go to that next level. "Grant that my sons may sit, on Your right hand and Your left, in Your kingdom." This was her prayer. The response, however, from Jesus was quick and to the point: "You don't know what you're asking," He implied that she was so focused on their promotion, she failed to recognize the process involved to get them there. There is always a process—a series of required steps that must be taken to achieve a particular end—and Jesus wanted her to understand there could be no promotion without a process.

First, Jesus said there is going to be a cup. It is the same cup His Father would give to Him in the Garden of Gethsemane. It was a cup of betrayal, humiliation, rejection and crucifixion. Second, Jesus referred to baptism. The baptism was His immersion into death and burial in the grave. In this metaphor, Jesus emphasized that before He could be promoted into that kingdom of the sons of Zebedee's affections, He would have to suffer, die and be resurrected—as would anyone who would join Him. "Be careful what you ask for," Jesus is saying to this mother, "What you're asking for requires a painful process because I won't promote them if they won't drink that cup."

What is perhaps even more revealing is the response of James and John. Jesus puts the question to them directly. He says, "Are you willing to drink the cup and suffer the baptism in order to get to that seat?" James and John, without hesitation—without a thought—say, "Yes, we are able."

This illustrates how we underestimate what it takes to get to the next level. "Sure! We can handle it. We can take it. We got this!" Too often we show no appreciation for the hardship and difficulty involved in the process. It's like enrolling in college without calculating the commitment, or getting married without embracing the selflessness, or having children without understanding the sacrifice. We want the degree, but not the long hours of study. We want companionship without selfless living. We want a happy home full of loving children, but not the midnight cries, dirty diapers, and sacrifice of personal comforts. But if we are to achieve those things (college degree, happy marriage, healthy children), there must be a death to who we are now and resurrection of a new person, with new attitudes and a new willingness to drink what's in the cup.

Jesus was telling them, there can be no crown without a cross, no chair without a cup and no resurrection without a crucifixion. He was saying, the promise requires a process. With every ascent, there will be some agony: if you want riches, you must experience poverty; if you want success, there will first be failure; if you want a higher level, you've got to face a higher devil. Between you and the seat, there will always be a cup.

I often ask my congregation, "How many want to go to the 'next level?" It's an ambiguous question, I know. But people apply it to whatever situation they are in—spiritually, financially, physically—most of us are eager to imagine ourselves at a much better place than we currently find ourselves. But after the hands go up and everyone shouts "Amen!" I follow up with another question: "Are you sure?" And again: "Are you really sure you want to go the next level?" I force the question because it's vital to know that God often has a much different idea, not only of what the next level looks like, but how we get there.

Here's the truth, the way to the next level is a struggle. It's a difficult journey. There's no quick prayer, no anointing and certainly no magic broom. If you want to be more effective, there will be struggle. If you want to be more successful, there will be a struggle. If you want to be happier, healthier and even holier, there will be a struggle because you can't have fulfillment, satisfaction or any kind of success in life without facing hardship along the way.

Anyone who has experienced success, anyone who has mastered some aptitude or achieved some level of greatness, at some point, on some level, had to face the struggle. One cannot succeed without it. Hard work, self-denial, sacrifice, adversity, suffering, loss, rejection—it's part of the journey, it's part of the process. The difference between those who are crushed by the process and those who are empowered by it is the theme of this book.

The character qualities that propel us to the next level—excellence, diligence, mental toughness, competence, moral virtue, and people skills—are so vital to our ascent that if they could be packaged and sold, the masses would pay dearly for them. But they cannot be packaged, nor can they be bought. The false prophets and fake preachers will tell you they have it in their bottles of oil and miracle hankies, but it's a sham. If you want to go to the next level, it requires hard work, determination and even suffering.

It's the kind of struggle that produces a certain kind of wisdom and strength that people who make it to the next level have. That's why we want to go there. We see the caliber and quality of people at that level and we want to be like them. But what we don't see is the struggle that got them there. The long days and sleepless nights, the countless tears and fears of the unknown, the cost, the sacrifice, the pressure and the pain. It was the struggle that made them wise, it was the fight that made them strong, it was the journey that forged their confidence that those below so eagerly admire.

This is not a book of formulas and instructions and seven steps to success. There's no such thing. Life has no simple equations. It's not a math problem that can be resolved with a few common rules that apply to everyone. It's not two plus two equals promotion, do this and that and you will succeed. No.

Each person's journey is unique. Your journey will be different than mine. Going to the next level is messy. There are no easy roads, no quick fixes, so don't think this book is going to make you succeed. It won't. Such are the expectations of the lazy mind.

What this book will do is push you forward. It will remind you that with each step you take there will be challenges, even pain, but you can push through it. With every move forward, there will be resistance and setbacks, but, with resilience, you can overcome. There will be enemies, both known and unknown, but greater is He that is in you. This book is your cheerleader, your coach, your reminder that the best is yet to come.

The words of the Apostle Paul from Philippians 3:21-14 make it clear:

> *"Not that I have already attained, or am already perfected; but I press on, that I may lay hold of that for which Christ Jesus has also laid hold of me. Brethren, I do not count myself to have apprehended; but one thing I do, forgetting those things which are behind and reaching forward to those things which are ahead, I press toward the goal for the prize of the upward call of God in Christ Jesus."*

The "next level" is not an overused cliché of self-help gurus and motivational moguls. For Paul, it was a way of life—it was his daily ascent. Never was he content with what he had achieved or how far he had come. Paul was always going higher, achieving more. He did not want to pass from this life with things undone. He wanted to reach the full potential of his existence, to achieve every purpose for which he was created.

There is untapped potential in your life. There is another level for you to achieve. Too many pass from this life believing the lie that they "can't" or they are "not good enough." Let the journey to fulfill your purpose begin now. Embrace the struggle and realize that there is a life you have yet to live, a joy you have yet to know. The joy of overcoming, achieving, pushing through, and accomplishing what you never thought possible and what everyone knew you could never do. For there's no greater joy than doing what everyone thought was impossible, if we do it for the glory of God.

CHAPTER ONE

EXCELLENCE

> **"** ***Opportunity does not simply appear. It is provoked by excellence.***

The story is told of a boy who found an eagle's egg on the forest floor. Unable to return the egg to its mother, he put it in the nest of a prairie chicken who accepted it as one of her own. Eventually the eagle hatched from its shell and grew up the community of little prairie chickens.

All his life, the eagle believed he was just another chicken. Sure, he looked different, walked different and sounded different, but that didn't matter. He knew he was a chicken and so he did what all good chickens do. He scavenged the dirt for insects and seeds. He clucked and crackled and twitched his large white head and hid from the predators above. On occasion he would flutter his wings and hover a few feet off the ground. But no more than that, for that's how prairie chickens were supposed to fly.

After several years among the chickens, the eagle, now much older, happened to see a magnificent bird flying far above him in the sky. With admiration he watched as this beautiful creature seemed to hang among the clouds with graceful majesty on the powerful currents of wind.

"What an extraordinary bird," the eagle-chicken said to his fellow prairie chickens. "What is it?" "That is an eagle, the king of birds," they replied. "But you could never be like him. You're a chicken!" they told him. So the earth-bound eagle never gave it another thought. He lived the rest of his life, and died, thinking he was nothing more than a chicken.[1]

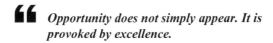

What a tragedy for the eagle. He was designed for greatness, built to soar—to rule the heavens. But he never got off the ground. Instead, he spent his life scratching in the dust for bugs and kernels, never even dreaming of soaring above the mountains.

It's the story of so many—not eagles, but people. It's what happens when we settle for a life among the chickens. We accept limitations where God never intended they should be and miss the greater purpose for which we were created.

Perhaps it's your story. Perhaps you feel as though you were meant for something greater—a purpose far greater than what you have achieved. You have a yearning to excel beyond ordinary and to surpass a mediocre existence that has kept you grounded, dwelling among the chickens.

An Eagle Among Chickens

When considering excellence, no example is more prominent that the Prophet Daniel. He is described as one who "*distinguished himself above the governors and satraps, because an excellent spirit was in him*" (Daniel 6:3). He was an eagle among chickens and provides us with a character study of one who aspires to excellence even in the most adverse conditions.

Daniel lived in Babylon. In 610 BC, he was taken from his homeland of Jerusalem and forced to live among the pagans. In Daniel Chapter 1, we see him refusing to defile himself with the king's delicacies and negotiated the approval of a diet more consistent with his Jewish convictions. The result was a healthier mind, a heartier countenance, and the favor of his handlers. Although he had been forced from his nest, to live among chickens, this eagle refused to diminish his identity to that of a chicken.

Over the course of his life, the eagle would soar. He demonstrated excellence in everything he did. As a result, he was distinguished with such significance that even "*the king gave thought to setting him over the whole realm*" (Daniel 6:3). The lesson is clear. In an environment where the prevailing attitude is mediocrity, excellence brings promotion. It will take you to the next level.

Before we consider the specifics of excellence as revealed the life of Daniel, we must first understand what excellence is and why it is important in our ascent to the next level.

Excellence in "Whatever You Do"

Excellence is not an option. We are called to it. The Apostle Paul constantly reminds us that one's highest effort should be seen in "*whatever you do*."

> "*Therefore, whether you eat or drink, or whatever you do, do all to the glory of God.*" - 1 Corinthians 10:31

> "*And whatever you do in word or deed, do all in the name of the Lord Jesus, giving thanks to God the Father through Him.*" - Colossians 3:17

> "*And whatever you do, do it heartily, as to the Lord and not to men.*" - Colossians 3:23

Excellence is not optional because the God we serve is a Being of omnipotent excellence. Isaiah 12:5 tells us, "*He has done excellent things.*" Psalm 150:2 extols, "*His excellent greatness!*" In all creation, we see His love of beauty and detail. The Creator did not haphazardly throw together a bleak, mediocre world made only from dull, grey matter having only base necessities to support life. The world He created is filled with incredible, excellent beauty. Majestic snowcapped mountains, strikingly exotic vegetation, fathomless oceans teeming with colorful varieties of life, dazzling sunsets, and starlit skies all demonstrate the reality that God loves beauty and excellence, and fine, crisp detail. Having realized this, the Psalmist proclaimed, "*O Lord, our Lord, how excellent is Your name in all the earth!*" (Psalm 8:9).

The excellence of the Creator is further seen in His dealings with mankind. With excellent detail, He gave Moses descriptions of the tabernacle. He inspired excellence in David, with which he developed and organized his government. Solomon showed excellence in the construction of the Lord's Temple. From the prophets to the poets to the splendor of Paul's epistles, every detail is articulated with divine excellence and beauty. Not to mention the intricate and excellent design of the human body. From the complexities of the eye to the engineering marvels of the ear, the psalmist declared, "*I am fearfully and wonderfully made; marvelous are Your works, and that my soul knows very well*" (Psalm 139:14). It's no wonder that we, as followers of this God of excellence, are commanded to "*approve the things that are excellent*" (Philippians 1:10).

Unfortunately, we live in a world where excellence is not the norm, mediocrity is. It's in the workplace, the church, the government, the military, the arts, and even athletics. Mediocrity is everywhere. In his book *The Screwtape Letters*, C.S. Lewis saw the demise of excellence as the devil's handiwork. His fictional demon named Screwtape said, "What I want to fix your attention on, is the vast, overall movement toward the discrediting, and finally the elimination, of every kind of human excellence—moral, cultural, social or intellectual."[2]

Simply look around. Many people today do as little as possible to get by. They don't take pride in their work, how they look, or the image they project. When people are watching them, they may perform one way, but when no one is watching, they cut corners and take the easy way out. Even worse, this attitude of indifference is contagious. It's like a disease that spreads through a culture like a toxic virus devouring its host. Those who work hard and strive for excellence become targets of the virus, attacked for being perfectionists or over-achievers. Forced to abandon their high standards, they succumb to a culture of ordinary, and become eagles living among chickens.

But for those who would soar, for those who cannot be content scratching in the dirt for insects and seeds, the pursuit of excellence is not an option. For those who are serious about the "next level," excellence must be more than a cliché—it must be a driving conviction, a persistent attitude, a mentality that invades everything they do.

Defining Excellence

In the words of Aristotle: "Excellence is an art won by training and habituation. We are what we repeatedly do. Excellence, then, is not an act but a habit." There is a reason why mediocrity is so popular: excellence is hard. If it was easy, everyone would be exceptional. The very nature of excellence is to excel, to be better than ordinary. A more specific definition is this: "Excellence is the discipline of consistently performing toward the upper range of your talent and skill beyond accepted levels of mediocrity." From this truth, we understand three things about excellence.

First, excellence is a discipline. It does not come naturally. Excellence does not "just happen." It's a condition we force upon ourselves—a discipline. Merriam-Webster defines discipline as "training that corrects, molds, or perfects the mental faculties or moral character."[3]

Discipline is the athlete who spends hours and hours in the gym perfecting certain routines and motions. Discipline is the student reading and rereading, memorizing and recalling new facts and information to master a certain subject. Discipline is the musician who rehearses hours on end to train his or her fingers in the proper motions. In each of these examples, the one in training is forcing himself or herself to act outside of their ordinary boundaries—to do something that is above normal or beyond ordinary to them. This is the beginning of excellence: to push beyond ordinary and consistently force ourselves beyond what is easy or comfortable. Those who cannot do that are destined to meander in a maze of mediocrity.

Second, excellence is to consistently perform toward the upper range of your talent and skill. In other words, excellence pushes your limits. It stretches you. It forces you to do and be better.

This is not to suggest that excellence requires perfection. Rather, excellence is about giving your best. Perfection, on the other hand, is about being flawless. It's about delivering a faultless, perfect product. Excellence isn't about the product, it's about the performance. It's not about winning, it's about giving your absolute best effort—performing toward the upper range of your skill. The reality is, one can play his or her best game. They can give their best effort, but still not have best score. In fact, they could lose. So, excellence is not about first place, second place, or even third place. Excellence is about work ethic.

Moreover, it's about consistent work ethic. Anyone can do their best, once in a while, especially when someone is watching them. But true excellence is what happens in the dark, when there's no spotlight and no one is watching. It's a sense of responsibility that obligates you to offer your absolute best effort in every situation regardless of who is watching, how much you're being paid, or who is going to know about it. Excellence says, "It's up to me to put forth an effort that makes a difference, and if I don't perform at my absolute best, then I am responsible for the failure that results."

Third, excellence is consistent performance beyond accepted levels of mediocrity. It refuses to settle for ordinary, even when ordinary is the prevailing mindset of the people around us.

There will always be chickens who try to discourage the eagle from flying. Friends that won't help you climb will want you to crawl. This is what average, mediocre people do; they try to increase their own sense of worth by diminishing the worth of others. They resent those who excel because it exposes their own lack of excellence. This is why eagles—if they are going to soar—can't fly with chickens.

At some point your pursuit of excellence will require you to disassociate with certain people—especially people who believe mediocre is "good enough." Colin Powell, retired four-star General and U.S. Secretary of State is quoted as saying, "The less you associate with some people, the more your life will improve. It's a simple but true fact of life; we become like those with whom we most closely associate, for the good and the bad. Any time you tolerate mediocrity in others, it increases your mediocrity."[4]

An important discipline of successful people is discretion in their choice of associates. They don't surround themselves with people that simply make them feel good by affirming their status quo. They surround themselves with possibility thinkers—people that challenge them. If you're serious about the next level, stop associating with people who are aiding and abetting your mediocrity. Yes, we need encouragement when we fail. Yes, we need friends who will inspire us to get up when we are down. But true inspiration and encouragement should never make an eagle feel content about living in a chicken coop. It should challenge him to see his own potential and God-given abilities. It should inspire him to get up and try again, to do better, to flap his wings harder, to fly longer, to expect more from himself until he achieves what God has created him to do.

Having defined and established its necessity in our lives, we return to Daniel for a practical example of how excellence can be cultivated and demonstrated in our everyday lives.

Excellence Begins with a Sense of Purpose

Daniel's excellence rose from a sense about himself. He knew he wasn't a Babylonian, he knew he was an Israelite, a son of David, a child of Abraham, a member of God's covenant people. From that awareness of his purpose he could never accept being a Babylonian. In Daniel 1:8 we read, "*Daniel purposed in his heart that he would not defile himself with the portion of the king's delicacies, nor with the wine which he drank...*" It was not that he thought himself to be better, he just knew that he was created for a specific purpose. And it was this sense of purpose that empowered him to stand apart.

When you know what your purpose is, you can never settle for being something other than what you know you were created to be. The king's delicacies will seem repulsive. On the other hand, people who have no sense of purpose will eat anything. They spend their lives conforming to some idea of greatness they have seen in others—or have been told by others that it's what they should do. Even if that to which they aspire is a noble thing, even if it's an achievement highly regarded and brings fame and fortune, if it does not align with one's purpose, it's nothing more than an eagle trying to be a chicken.

On an episode of *American Idol*, where amateur vocalists compete for recording contracts, Simon Cowell, one of the show's judges, told a contestant, "Are you taking singing lessons? Who's your teacher? Do you have a lawyer? Get a lawyer and sue her."

I agree, it was cruel. But why would someone with such an unpleasant singing voice actually believe she should compete on a national level, on an internationally televised event? Obviously, no one ever told that young contestant the truth: She did not have a talent for singing. She was created to soar, but it wasn't singing that would give her lift—it was something else. Unfortunately, she would never know how to fly because she wanted to be something she wasn't created to be. She would rather be a mediocre singer—she would rather be a chicken.

Years ago, in a church where I served as youth pastor, a woman sang a song, accompanied by her son on the piano. It was among the most unpleasant sounds I ever heard. The song itself was beautiful—an old hymn of the church written for the glory of God. But she turned it into a dreadful shrill of vibrato that nearly peeled the paint off the walls. Not only was it off key, it was painfully embarrassing. It seemed everyone in the room knew how awful her singing was, except her. But we were nice people, so we patiently endured the melodic misery until her indulgence was complete.

As a young pastor-in-training, I wondered why someone would be permitted to stand before a group of people, screech out some noise and call it singing—or even "worship"? Some will say, "Well, it's a 'joyful noise.' Any praise to God, no matter how badly it sounds, is lovely to Him." Sure, I believe that. If someone sings to the Lord in their private time, or as part of congregational praise, God is not concerned about their key, pitch, or tone. He just loves their worship. But when an individual is given a responsibility to lead in a way that requires a certain level of proficiency and aptitude, they should perform at a level commensurate to the task.

If I take my child to a doctor, I expect that doctor to be excellent. The fact that "the doctor has a good heart" does not matter if she makes my child's condition worse. If I hire a carpenter to build a house, I don't care how much "doing woodwork fulfills him." I want to know that the walls are plumb and the floors are level. If they aren't, he will be fired and not paid. We demand excellence in the things that benefit us. We want the best cars, the best phones, the best computers, and the best athletes for our favorite teams, but in the things that matter to God—and even in what we offer to Him—mediocrity is good enough.

Today, excellence is being replaced with emotional egalitarianism. In other words, we don't mind lowering standards of performance as long as everybody gets to participate and feels good. In this calculus, what matters most is self-esteem. Untalented, ungifted people get to do what makes them feel satisfied, despite how unpleasant the experience is for a hundred others who have to follow them. We tell ourselves, "God gave Mary a song and we love Mary. Mary has such a good heart, so let's have Mary sing." So Mary gets up on Sunday morning and screeches out her "God-song." The intent is not to honor God with a song of excellence, the intent is to make Mary feel good. However, what needs to happen, is someone must love Mary enough to inform her that she may have a gift for writing songs, but she certainly doesn't have a gift for singing them.

There's nothing more troubling than to watch an eagle aspire to be a chicken. The eagle is created for something different (and for him, that means something greater), but he has convinced himself that he should be clucking and crowing and scratching the dirt. Unfortunately, as an eagle, he'll never be a great chicken. He can crow and cluck all day long, but he was not created for that purpose. And until he embraces his true purpose and seeks to excel in that, he will always be a mediocre, even substandard, strange-looking, strange-sounding chicken.

If you want to be an eagle, if you want to go the next level, stop trying to be a chicken. Stop trying to fit into a role that wasn't meant for you. Learn what God has gifted you for, develop those gifts, excel in those abilities, and see how you soar. Through the years, I have known scores of people who had a passion about something, but it wasn't their purpose. I've seen singers, leaders, church planters, preachers, athletes, and teachers who were sincere and passionate, but they could never excel—they were bad at what they did. Passion is not enough; you must know your purpose.

I wanted to be a worship leader. I played the guitar, I sang the newest, trendiest worship songs. But I lacked one thing: a singer's vocal chords. Sure, I could lead worship if I had to. Anyone can lead worship if they have to. But that doesn't mean it will be good. In fact, if you're not suited for singing, it will be bad. In fact, it could be so bad it's a hindrance and distraction from worship. So, having discovered that my gifting was not in singing or worship leading, I learned that my gifting is in leadership and pastoral ministry. My goal was not to be an excellent chicken—I mean worship leader—it was to be an excellent pastoral leader who could identify and raise up those whose purpose is to sing and lead worship. Now, God has taken me to a whole new level of being able to recognize potential in others, developing that potential, and releasing them into ministry—especially worship leading.

That's not to imply that being a worship leader is being a chicken. It's only "being a chicken" to those that are designed for another purpose. When you're fulfilling your God-given purpose, you're soaring like an eagle. When you're trying to be something God never intended, you're clucking with the chickens.

God created you to soar—to be an eagle. But first, you must discover what kind of an eagle. Don't try to be a singer, if you're gifted as an administrator. Don't try to be a church planter, if you're gifted as an accountant. Don't try to be a preacher, if you're gifted as a carpenter. Be a great carpenter, be a great accountant, be a great administrator. Develop excellence in your God-given skills and see how God will promote you.

Excellence Distinguishes Those Who Possess It

Daniel was distinguished "*because an excellent spirit was in him.*" As a result, "*the king gave thought to setting him over the whole realm*" (Daniel 6:3). In an environment where the prevailing attitude is mediocrity, excellence brings distinction and distinction brings promotion.

Excellence brings distinction because it reflects the character of God. If you desire God's favor in the workplace or anyplace, it does not come because you're deeply spiritual or have some ambiguous "anointing to prosper." God's favor comes upon those who "*order their conduct aright*" (Psalm 50:23) and demonstrate practical righteousness (Psalm 5:12). In so doing, they give silent witness to the nature and character of God. One's spirituality and gospel witness may be important, but in the workplace, value is measured in a pragmatic way.

If you're a carpenter, what good is your witnessing if the customer you shared the gospel with buys a chair from you, takes it home, sits on it, and the chair collapses. If you're a mechanic, what good is handing out gospel tracts if the car belonging to the patron, whom you give a tract to, breaks down three miles down the road. If you're a teacher, what good are all your prayers for all your students if you come to class with a bad attitude, scream at the children, and tell little Johnny he is a loser. Whatever your position or job title, what good is your "spirituality" if you're gossiping, cursing, complaining, showing up late, leaving early and, by default, forcing everyone else do your work.

When our work product is poor, or mediocre at best, our witness becomes a reproach on God. Mediocrity associates the Creator who is high, holy, and perfect with poor, lazy, and sloppy performance. 1 Peter 2:12 reminds us to have "*your conduct honorable among the Gentiles, that when they speak against you as evildoers, they may, by your good works which they observe, glorify God in the day of visitation.*"

By contrast, excellence brings glory to God and results in His blessing. In Matthew 5:16, Jesus said, "*Let your light so shine before men, that they may see your good works and glorify your Father in heaven.*" When coworkers see your hard work and productivity, it glorifies God. When you develop a new product or new initiative, it glorifies God. When you coach the team to a winning season, it glorifies God. When your boss uses you as an example of success, it glorifies God. The fact is, our lives should glorify God more out in the world than inside the church. Most Christians know that God is great as we lift up His praises in the sanctuary, but when your teammate or coworker compliments you for a job well done, it speaks well of your character and of the God you serve. Your excellence causes the heathen to praise the Lord and God will bless you. This is why Deuteronomy 28:1-5 tells us:

> "*Now it shall come to pass, if you diligently obey the voice of the LORD your God, to observe carefully all His commandments which I command you today, that the LORD your God will set you high above all nations of the earth. And all these blessings shall come upon you and overtake you, because you obey the voice of the LORD your God: Blessed shall you be in the city, and blessed shall you be in the country. Blessed shall be the fruit of your body, the produce of your ground and the increase of your herds, the increase of your cattle and the offspring of your flocks. Blessed shall be your basket and your kneading bowl.*"

Excellence brings distinction because authorities look for excellence in the people they promote. Proverbs 22:29 says, "*Do you see a man who excels in his work? He will stand before kings; He will not stand before unknown men.*"

I often hear employees say, "Pay me more money so I can do a better job." It's a common misconception of mediocre mindset: "I can produce more, but you have to reward me first." It's a sense of entitlement—a belief that I deserve to be paid at a higher level than I currently produce. But real life doesn't work that way. What I tell employees is this: "Do better work, show me how valuable you are, demonstrate how indispensable you are, and then I'll pay you more." Notice the progression—first excel in your work, demonstrate excellence, and then you will stand before kings.

Booker T. Washington said, "Excellence is to do a common thing in an uncommon way." In other words, the work you have been given, although it's common, mundane and boring, if done with uncommon effort will stand apart. Like Daniel, it will bring respect, distinguish your character, and open doors.

One of my sons landed a temporary job with Federal Express over the Christmas season. Due to the increased volume of shipping during this holiday, they hired a small army of part-time employees. My son had hopes of continuing his employment beyond that temporary season and securing a full-time job. Not once did he say to his managers, "Give me a full-time job and you'll really see how good I am." No, instead he excelled in his work. He showed up early, stayed late, produced three times more than the other temps, loaded one truck by himself whereas other trucks required teams of two or three. He demonstrated excellence in his attitude, work ethic, and productivity. The result? My son was offered a full-time job with Federal Express proving the proverb: *If one excels in his work, he will be promoted.*

You have to be something more to get something more. You have to increase your value to create more opportunities. Don't whine that you never get more hours, or wish you had a higher position. Instead, produce at the level for which you're aiming and make yourself indispensable. When the time comes for promotions, your name will be at the top of the list.

Excellence brings distinction because excellence brings honor to those who walk in it. Proverbs 22:1 tells us, "*A good name is to be chosen rather than great riches, loving favor rather than silver and gold.*" The greatest asset any man or woman has is not their talent, their resources or even their family heritage. Your greatest asset is your name, your reputation.

There are those who ignorantly say, "I don't care what people think about me. I'm my own person, I do as I please and people's opinions don't matter." While that may sound daring, it's actually quite foolish. Having a good name is not about needing people's affirmation to feel good about one's self. Being a people pleaser is unhealthy and betrays a deep seated insecurity. To have a good name, on the other hand, is to be a person of honor.

Honor is about character. It's the bestowment of respect to a man or woman by those in their society or group who share certain standards or values. If you're a part of a particular group or community, then honor is something you care about. It means that within that society of shared values, you have a reputation of respect and admiration, based upon your performance of those values. It means the people with whom you work can count on you. They see your value and want you on their team. You're held in high regard. It's called honor.

It's why the military awards medals to those within their ranks. It's why athletic leagues give trophies to teams that excel. It's why companies give bonuses and special amenities to those who achieve, and schools recognize those who advanced in academics. We honor those among us who excel, or at least we should. Unfortunately, when we dumb down education so everyone student receives a passing grade regardless of their performance and every team "wins" a trophy even though most of them were inferior, we undermine our society's sense of honor and diminish the value of excellence.

The reality is, despite egalitarian activists, the real world is ruled by such blatant concepts as win or lose and fail or succeed. And in this world, a good name matters. Honor makes the difference.

At the time of this writing, the Internet company eBay announced it will be cutting 2,400 jobs. American Express is cutting 4,000 jobs. U.S. oil services group Baker Hughes & Halliburton will lay off 8,000 employees and the energy and technology giant Schlumberger will cut 9,000 jobs.[5] Signaling additional potential cuts, Apple, the manufacturer of iPhone, has forecast its first sales decline since 2003 following its slowest-ever rise in iPhone shipments amid weakening demand.[6] Regardless of how well a company may be doing today, it will inevitably encounter challenging times. Declines in sales, tragic loss, mergers, restructuring could happen at any time forcing an employer to make cuts in their work force. This means layoffs. But who will be laid off and why? What are the factors that determine if one would keep or lose his job? One of the most important factors is his or her name—their reputation.

A recent report done by Becker's ASC Review revealed the top five performance issues that lead to being fired. The first is sloppy work product. Employees who cut corners, produce careless results, and fall short of delivering an efficient, properly executed work product are at the top of the list to go. They fail to upgrade themselves and thereby become obsolete. They lack versatility in their core competences and grow complacent in their comfort zone.

Second on the list are those who disregard company policies and do things "their own way." These are the people who ignore their supervisor's instructions or appropriate protocol and take short cuts and bypass essential metrics, thinking their way is better (or more convenient for them).

Then there are those with attitude issues. Despite having talent or being highly skilled, those who have a generally poor attitude become low hanging fruit. Complaining, spreading discontentment among workers, gossiping, and contributing to a low morale in the work environment is what managers despise most.

A fourth performance issue that leads to dismissal is tardiness and attendance inconsistency. Arriving late, getting to meetings late, or consistent absence from, or lateness to, required duties is certain to get you fired.

The fifth issue is employee conflicts and disputes. Employers put high value on being able to work well with and get along with others. When companies face cutbacks, those who are abrasive, create friction, and lack people skills will quickly find themselves filing for unemployment.[7]

Do you have a good name? When management evaluates you, what will come to mind? Hopefully, you would be known for a positive attitude, versatility in your skill sets, one who improves one's competencies and inspires others to a higher level. A good name comes from excellence and will bring promotion to your life.

Excellence Comes from Wisdom

One essential factor that contributed to Daniel's reputation of a man with "an excellent spirit" was his wisdom. When King Belshazzar was confronted by a divine hand, writing on the wall, he fell into despair because no one in the kingdom could interpret the heavenly script. The queen, upon hearing this dilemma, said to the king:

> "*O king, live forever! Do not let your thoughts trouble you, nor let your countenance change. There is a man in your kingdom in whom is the Spirit of the Holy God. And in the days of your father, light and understanding and wisdom, like the wisdom of the gods, were found in him; and King Nebuchadnezzar your father—your father the king—made him chief of the magicians, astrologers, Chaldeans, and soothsayers. Inasmuch as an excellent spirit, knowledge, understanding, interpreting dreams, solving riddles, and explaining enigmas were found in this Daniel, whom the king named Belteshazzar, now let Daniel be called, and he will give the interpretation.*" - Daniel 5:10-12

Clearly, the excellence for which Daniel was known was connected to the wisdom that others perceived in him. "Light and understanding and wisdom, like the wisdom of the gods, were found in him," is what the queen said. He was excellent because he was wise.

In order for wisdom to be present, it requires three components: knowledge, understanding, and action. Knowledge is simply the possession of facts. For example, knowledge tells me that my car is almost out of gas. Understanding takes that awareness deeper. It reasons and calculates and knows what those facts will produce. In other words, if I continue driving with such a small amount of gas, I will eventually run out and be stranded on the road. Knowledge sees the "dots," but understanding connects those dots and foresees an outcome. Wisdom, however, takes these two functions even further.

Wisdom is the ability to see the dots connected and know what to do about it. It thinks through the complexities of a situation and formulates an appropriate response. It recognizes the converging dynamics upon a circumstance and acts to minimize damage and maximize benefits. In other words, if I read the dashboard instruments and see my gas tank is almost empty—that's knowledge. The realization that if I keep driving, I will be stranded, is understanding. Wisdom, however, acts on that understanding. It says, "I will alter my course and speed, find a gas station and fill my tank." That's wisdom.

Wisdom has insight, foresight, and acts right. Wisdom is hindsight before it becomes hindsight. Wisdom anticipates and projects. It plans and prepares. Proverbs 22:3 says, "*A prudent (wise) man foresees evil and hides himself, but the simple pass on and are punished.*" Proverbs 14:16 tells us, "*A wise man fears and departs from evil, but a fool rages and is self-confident.*" An excellent spirit is demonstrated by the capacity to understand certain circumstances and avoid trouble.

I know two young men. One is thoughtful and deliberate. He is not driven by impulse and what-feels-good-right-now. He is willing to delay gratification in order to achieve long term gain. He works hard, earns money, saves money, avoids drugs, obeys authority, and worships God. As a result, the people around him see him as a person of worth and value. He is respected and sought out by leaders who want him on his team. Why? Because he has an excellent spirit—a spirit of wisdom.

The second young man is different. He is more concerned about immediate gratification and having fun right now. He doesn't value hard work, so he complains and finds the easy way out. He likes alcohol, experiments with drugs, and gets in trouble in school. As a result, he is not respected by others and is regarded as a low value person. Why? Because he does not have an excellent spirit—he lacks wisdom.

So where does wisdom come from? Can a person gain more wisdom than she currently has? Absolutely. The Bible is a book of wisdom and shows us three simple ways this virtue is obtained.

First, wisdom comes from God. Psalm 111:10 says, "*The fear of the Lord is the beginning of wisdom.*" Proverbs 2:6-7 tells us, "*The Lord gives wisdom, from His mouth come knowledge and understanding. He stores up sound wisdom for the upright.*" The mind that has been instructed in the Word of God and enlightened by the Spirit of God and walks in relationship with God will have knowledge, understanding and wisdom. There will be an ability to discern and understand, to connect the dots and anticipate danger. There will also be a sense of discipline and the delay of gratification for long term gain. Such is the character of a person who has been regenerated by the Holy Spirit and displaying spiritual fruitfulness.

Even more, James 1:5 reminds us, "*If any of you lacks wisdom, let him ask of God, who gives to all liberally and without reproach, and it will be given to him.*" God promises to answer the prayer for wisdom. Like any good Father who is overjoyed by a child asking for good gifts, He loves to give wisdom. Pray and ask God and see what He does. The prayer for wisdom will always be answered, and the seeds of an excellent spirit will be planted.

Second, wisdom comes from man. While God promises to provide wisdom, it's important to understand how He does it. The answer does not come in the form of a larger brain that is bigger, faster, and smarter. No. Typically, God answers the prayer for wisdom by making the people around you smarter. If you're a pastor, your deacons will get smarter. If you're a business man, your board will be wiser. If you're a student, your teachers will get brighter. They key is this: Will you be humble enough to receive the wisdom God has for you by allowing them to teach, advise, and speak into you?

Consider the Proverbs: 8:33 says, "*Hear instruction and be wise;*" 10:17 tells us, "*He who keeps instruction is in the way of life, but he who refuses correction goes astray;*" 15:32 warns, "*He who disdains instruction despises his own soul, but he who heeds rebuke gets understanding.*" Clearly, God's plan for giving wisdom includes our willingness to be instructed and taught by others. This is why Proverbs 11:14 says, "*Where there is no counsel, the people fall, but in the multitude of counselors there is safety.*" Those who can take advice, hear criticism, and receive instruction will receive the wisdom that God promises to provide because He provides it by way of our humility. Humble yourselves in the sight of the Lord and He will exalt you. Indeed, wisdom provides us with an excellent spirit, but humility is a doorway through which that wisdom comes.

Third, wisdom comes from experience. The man with a scar is wiser than the man with a warning. Everything that hurts us, teaches us.

John Wimber said, "I don't trust any leader that doesn't walk with a limp." A.W. Tozer wrote, "It's doubtful whether God can bless a man greatly until He has hurt him deeply." Pain always brings the greatest wisdom.

In his book, *Leadership Pain,* Sam Chand wrote, "When you're born, you're like a key with no cuts in it. As you go through life, each wound, failure, hurt cuts into that strip of metal. And one day there is a clear click—your pain has formed the key that slips into the lock and opens your future. Chand goes on to say, "The pain we experience in the first forty years of our lives gives us the wisdom and experience for a far more profound ministry for the rest of our lives."[8]

There is an unfortunate trend in many American churches that are searching for a new pastor. Many of them want young, trendy individuals, rather than more experienced, mature leaders. Not only is this true in churches, it reflects a greater norm in our culture.

A recent survey of young professionals aged 18-25 revealed that youth today really don't value experience. Sixty-four percent believe the ideal leader is under the age of 40. Only about half (56 percent) thought age was a valuable factor in leadership, while only 33 percent felt that experience was most important.[9] It's unfortunate. Many people today (not only youth) believe style and trendiness is more valuable than experience and history. The result is often an organization that lacks depth and the capacity to process a complex and highly nuanced strategy.

In military units, the opposite is usually true. It's not usually the young lieutenant that is sought out for advice when developing a mission; it's the N.C.O.—the older, war-torn sergeant who carries deep scars and a rough demeanor he earned on the battlefield. Every team has a sergeant and the troops usually look to him because they know he has "earned his stripes." His experience makes his opinion much more valuable than the fresh-out-of-West-Point lieutenant.

Excellence Comes from Integrity

Daniel's excellence resulted in great favor from the king. He considering making him second in the kingdom. As a result, all Daniel's colleagues became jealous and wanted to ruin his credibility. As they sought ways to do this, something very important was revealed about his character. Daniel 6:4 says, "*The governors and satraps sought to find some charge against Daniel concerning the kingdom; but they could find no charge or fault, because he was faithful; nor was there any error or fault found in him.*" Daniel's excellent spirit was a function of his exceptional integrity.

This is revealed further when God spoke through the prophet Ezekiel regarding the destruction of Israel. He said, "*Even if these three men, Noah, Daniel, and Job, were in it, they would deliver only themselves by their righteousness, says the Lord GOD*" (Ezekiel 14:14). Daniel's integrity was so great, God Himself numbered him among the most righteous.

Alan Simpson said, "If you have integrity, nothing else matters. If you don't have integrity, nothing else matters." In other words, gifting, talent, skill sets, and competencies are all important, but if a person lacks principles and a strong moral center, none of those things will sustain him.

Almost everyone has high regard for integrity until it costs them something personally. This is a day in which "the end justifies the means." In other words, it's perfectly reasonable to lie, cheat, and even steal, as long as some personal gain is received by doing so. Applicants lie on job applications because they desperately need a job. Students cheat on tests because the college scholarships require high grades. Sales people embellish and misrepresent the facts because they have to make a monthly quota. CEOs overstate their earnings because a hefty performance bonus awaits. Pastors exaggerate attendance because it brings them higher prestige. Employees call in sick because they want to spend the day at the beach with their families. The list could go on and on, and every person who lies, cheats, and steals has a "perfectly valid reason" why they should do so—or so they think.

Unfortunately, every time we compromise our integrity for personal gain, we cheapen ourselves and diminish our excellence. Sure, we may receive some instant gratification from our compromise, but the long-term effects are far costlier than we realize.

First, with every breach of integrity comes a diminished sense of personal excellence. After one lie is told, the next lie is easier, and the next and the next, until lying is something that can be done without regret. We become desensitized to the guilt. Yes, guilt. Guilt can be a good thing when it comes in the form of remorse and regret for some immoral action. People of conviction and principle feel guilt when they have violated those principles. They feel ashamed and embarrassed. This kind of guilt is healthy. It comes from integrity and often drives people of excellence to a place of higher performance and trustworthiness. Eventually, their integrity propels them to the next level. On the contrary, people who lie, cheat, and steal (etc.) on a regular basis feel no guilt. Immorality, compromise, corruption comes easy to them. There is little internal drive to do good, be one's best and perform with an inner sense of pride and dignity from simply doing the right thing. Their lack of integrity diminishes their value and closes doors of opportunity.

Second, people who compromise integrity become known for their lack of excellence. It may appear as though one gains an advantage if he or she is willing to act without the constraints of morality, but a lack of integrity also brings a lack of credibility. Such people lose their ability to be trusted as men or women of character, which is the most valuable quality anyone can have in their life. Monetary profit is important, but it's never as important as one's reputation. Proverbs 22:1 tells us, "*A good name is to be chosen rather than great riches, loving favor rather than silver and gold.*"

People of integrity have powerful reputations. It's true in any field, any profession, any community. We love and respect people who can be trusted—and we want them on our team. For employers, it means a manager who can be trusted with more responsibilities and greater resources. For businesses, it means more clients who see them as reliable. For churches, it means communities that will respect and value them. For governments, it means constituencies who will support and honor them rather than scorn, ridicule, mock, and undermine them.

By contrast, when we know someone lacks integrity, we want nothing to do with them. We don't buy products from them. We don't do business with them. We don't go to their churches or send our children to their schools. We generally understand that if they were dishonest with others, they will be dishonest with us. Therefore, when we hear them lie, or see them cheat, or know that they steal, we don't dismiss, or make excuses for, those acts. We see them as indicators of that person's character. They cannot and should not be trusted, regardless of how successful, attractive, or famous they may be. Solomon said it well in Ecclesiastes 10:1, "*Dead flies putrefy the perfumer's ointment, and cause it to give off a foul odor; so does a little folly to one respected for wisdom and honor.*"

Third, people who lack integrity, tarnish the excellence of those closest to them. Be aware: Those with whom you associate will reflect back on you. Those who observe us, often judge our character by the company we keep. Sound unfair? Think people shouldn't "judge" you? Sorry, they do. In fact, studies show that these "judgments" are actually somewhat accurate. Many social observers believe we are the average of the five people with whom we spend the most time. This is why it has been said, "Show me your friends and I will show you your future. Show me the five people who are closest to you and I will show you what you will be five years from now." Additionally, this is why Proverbs 12:26 says, "*The righteous should choose his friends carefully, for the way of* *the wicked leads them astray*." Simply stated, we become more and more like the people with whom we surround ourselves. And people who are concerned about integrity know this is true.

Daniel was a man with an excellent spirit because he was a man of exceptional integrity. He had built a reputation for honesty, reliability, trustworthiness, and integrity. As a result, he was promoted to the second highest position of authority in the kingdom. If you want to be known as a person of excellence, if you want to go to the next level, start by excelling in integrity.

Excellence Comes from a Spiritual Life

Frustrated by their failure to find flaws in Daniel's integrity, the Satraps lamented, "*We shall not find any charge against this Daniel unless we find it against him concerning the law of his God*" (Daniel 6:5). The only plan they could muster was to force Daniel to defy the king's command by outlawing prayer. They knew that Daniel, a man devoted to his Faith, would never forfeit his communion with God. It was a testament to the value he placed on spiritual disciplines. In fact, it was this devotion to God's Word, regular prayer, and daily walking with God that made him excellent.

Being a Christian should make a person a better person. It should make a husband a better husband—and make a wife a better wife. Christianity should make employees into honest and diligent workers and civil servants into true servants of the people rather than crooks seeking personal gain.

Romans 14:12 says, "*Each of us shall give account of himself to God*." Hebrews 9:27 reminds us, "*It is appointed for men to die once, but after this the judgment*." The Christian's awareness of accountability to God is a driving motivation. Someone once asked Daniel Webster, "What is the greatest thought that you have ever had?" He said, "The most awesome, the most terrifying, the most shattering thought I've ever had, is my personal responsibility to God." It's true. Because I know that I will stand before God and give an account of my attitude, my work ethic and my pursuit of excellence, I am inspired to be the best husband, father, and pastor I can be. Remove this sense of divine accountability, and man has little reason to perform in life with excellence.

Excellence Comes from Sexual Purity

The book of Daniel indicates that some of the young Jewish captives, including Daniel and his three friends, were taken to Babylon and placed in the care of the "chief of the eunuchs" (Daniel 1:7). The Hebrew word is "*saris*." Although not exclusively, it was a word often used to describe a man who had been emasculated in order to fill a religious or governmental role, especially when serving in the king's court. This fact, along with the repeated prophecy of 2 Kings 20:18 and Isaiah 39:7 which says, "*They shall take away some of your sons who will descend from you, whom you will beget; and they shall be eunuchs in the palace of the king of Babylon*," seems likely that Daniel and his friends were made eunuchs by the Babylonians.

It begs an interesting question: If Daniel was a eunuch, how might this contribute to him having an excellent spirit? Perhaps this could be understood when considering the addictive tendency that unbridled sexual lust has over a man—especially as it relates to today's modern media plague: pornography.

Pornography has a corruptive, degenerative influence over a man's character. Porn, like no other medium, "rewires" the brain and creates a destructive cycle that is extremely difficult to escape. In many ways it acts like a drug. Although it's not a physical substance, pornography results in the same general loss of control and compulsiveness to seek it out again and again.[10]

Scientific research reveals that continued use of porn causes long term neuroplastic changes in the brain. Dopamine (a chemical in the brain) is released whenever we do something that "feels good," whether it be eating to sustain life or sexual activity meant to produce future life. This dopamine creates neural connections that drive us to perform the same activity in the future. In other words, it alters and forms the brain cells to motivate certain action. This is what occurs when porn stimulates the brain's pleasure centers—it rewires the brain.

Unfortunately, the more time spent with pornography, the more porn is required to get that dopamine release. Like an alcoholic who develops a tolerance for alcohol and requires more to get a buzz, porn users become desensitized to images that brought arousal and need more intense and graphic images to trigger the dopamine release. This is why porn addiction starts out as intermittent use of soft porn and gradually increases to hard porn, then to violent porn, even acting out violently or engaging in forms of perversion. Talk to anyone who is addicted to porn. They'll tell you it didn't start out that way. They started with viewing soft porn, but needed more and more. They even lost interest in their own spouse and needed more intense, graphic visual images to get turned on. It's called an addiction, an addiction to porn.

Sadly, one who has lost such control over himself is suffering a corrosion of character. And typically this corruption infects his potential for excellence in almost every area of his life. Discipline succumbs to gratification and healthy behavior is lost to repetitive cycles of unhealthy behavior which leave a person full of shame, regret, and self-loathing. Hardly the qualities that promote excellence in one's character.

Does this mean that excellence can only be obtained by becoming a eunuch? Of course not. It does suggest, however, that certain carnal influences must be eliminated in order to avoid the corruption of one's nature—especially as it relates to today's overtly promiscuous culture.

Today, we are inundated with offers of lust at every turn. Billboards, television, books, magazines, and, of course, the Internet provide an endless supply of sexual stimuli. For men, it usually involves pornographic pictures or video, whereas women are more susceptible to email entanglements and romantic social websites. Studies show that with unlimited access to the Internet, virtual sex is a ubiquitous epidemic polluting untold millions of minds and destroying thousands of families. Forget about excellence, sexual addiction is ruining lives.

Consider these facts. Every day, 200 new pornography websites are created. Seventy-five percent of hits on the Internet are looking for a porn site. The largest group of viewers of porn are boys between the age of 13 and 18 years old. Almost 90 percent of American teens view porn online. Ninety-four percent of men have been exposed to pornography before the age of 20.[11] The reality is this: A spirit overcome by sexual lust is not excellent. It's a spirit in bondage; a spirit in servitude to carnal impulse, out of control.

In some cases, prayer and repentance is not enough. Those who have a difficult time controlling their urges need to adopt a more aggressive plan for reclaiming their excellence. Typically, it requires a willingness to be accountable to others.

One study done at Dallas Theological Seminary examined 237 instances of Christians who suffered moral failure. One interesting commonality was revealed: Of the 237 men who fell, not one of them had accountability relationships with other men. If your excellence is waning because porn has rewired your brain, seriously consider confessing your struggle to an accountability partner you trust and allow him or her the right to speak into your life and question you on a regular basis. Having an accountability group or partner is not a sign of weakness—it's a sign of strength. It reveals a depth of character that refuses to compromise excellence.

Excellence Comes with Great Cost

Excellence almost killed him. More specifically, the people around Daniel who resented his excellence wanted him dead. The governors and satraps contrived a plan that forced Daniel to choose between his king and his God. No one was allowed to pray, except for the king. Disobey and you die. They knew Daniel would never compromise—it was part of his character, his excellence. Daniel would rather face a den of lions than sacrifice his integrity—and that is exactly what they were counting on.

> *"And they went before the king, and spoke concerning the king's decree: 'Have you not signed a decree that every man who petitions any god or man within thirty days, except you, O king, shall be cast into the den of lions?' So they answered and said before the king, "That Daniel, who is one of the captives from Judah, does not show due regard for you, O king, or for the decree that you have signed, but makes his petition three times a day."* - Daniel 6:12-13

It wasn't Daniel that the governors and satraps hated. They hated his excellence. They hated that his excellence distinguished him. They hated that his excellence promoted him and gave him exceptional favor with the king. His excellence was a threat to them. It made them look bad and feel bad about how they looked. The way Daniel lived, spoke, and carried himself was a reproach on their mediocrity.

There's a little known fact that the more successful you become—happier, healthier, more content—the more some people will resent you. They may not conspire to have you thrown into a den of lions, but that may only be because there are no lions available. The reality is many people simply cannot handle excellence in others. They love to be around the average, the low achiever, even the failure, because it makes them comfortable—by comparison, they feel pretty good about their mediocrity. But when they get around someone who pursues greatness, it makes them uncomfortable. They become critical, toxic, judgmental, and gossipy. Learn a lesson from Daniel: Be prepared for rejection on your journey to the next level. Here are six quick truths to bear in mind.

Some people will leave you. Don't worry, it's not the end of your story. It's just the end of their part in your story. Don't hold onto people who have let go of you. It cheapens you and makes you look like a victim, as though their approval has power over you. Realize that some relationships are for a season. They were there to help you get to a certain level, but what got you there can't get you to where you are going. Let go and move on.

Be kind to everyone you meet, for some are fighting a great battle. Realize that many with critical spirits are not reacting to you, they are reacting to the pain they have been carrying for years. For some, anger and confrontation are their comfort zones and they are not happy unless they are creating chaos. Don't be infected by their toxic attitude. Stay above the fray and demonstrate your excellence. Remain calm and be professional, and allow your excellent spirit to speak for itself.

Smile, not because you're happy, but because you're strong. Winston Churchill said, "I like a man who grins when he fights." Criticism can hurt. It's painful to be thrown to the lions, especially when you've done nothing wrong. But this is when excellence shines brightest. When everyone is against you and there seems to be no reason to hope—smile. Exude confidence and enthusiasm, not because you're enjoying the pain, but because you know greatness is in you and God is with you and He causes all things to work together for the good.

Insecure people try to increase their value by diminishing the worth of others. When people gossip and criticize you, when they mock and oppose you, it's often because your excellence is a threat to what they know about themselves. It's what a man believes about himself that often fuels his criticism of others. This is why so many people love to gossip and tear others down. Pointing out the flaws in those who excel, makes those who are average feel a little better about their own inadequacies. Always remember, the closer you get to excellence, the more friends you lose. People love average because it makes them comfortable.

Never comfort someone else's mediocrity by compromising your own excellence. Steve Jobs said, "Be a yardstick of quality. Some people aren't used to an environment where excellence is expected." The temptation is to lower our standards so people around us won't feel pressured or intimidated. Big mistake. We must choose between being accepted and fitting in, or being excellent and risking the lion's den. Most people want excellence—they respect it and respond to it. Unfortunately, they lack the capacity to provoke it in others. Be a leader who challenges status quo and incites excellence—and discover how your value increases.

Never allow the "virtue of authenticity" to become a celebration of mediocrity. It seems that today, "authenticity" is the new excellence. In other words, being flawed and failing is "in." You can underperform—and be sloppy, lazy, and weak—as long as you're "being true to yourself" and "not judging others." Excellence and confidence have become liabilities; we want people who are frail and vulnerable. While it's true that transparency and humility are essential qualities, we should never feel good about accepting mediocrity as normal. Neither should we project weakness in order to make a good impression. Everyone should do their best, be their best, and expect the best from others. This is not being judgmental, or critical, or a perfectionist—it's called "having standards." It's called excellence and it should be celebrated without apology.

A Word to the Governors and Satraps

Unfortunately, not everyone reading this will be a Daniel. In fact, the Daniels are usually the minority. Most people will be among the governors and satraps, standing on the sidelines hurling resentment at those who strive toward excellence. Which one are you? Are you a Daniel or a sideline critic looking for ways to throw excellence to the lions? You can always recognize the governors and satraps by three distinct attributes.

Do you have a critical spirit? If so, you've probably justified it by saying something like: "I'm just discerning" or "I tell it like it is." Perhaps you do have a discerning spirit, but do you mostly "discern" what is bad about someone rather than discerning what is good? Are you usually pointing out the negatives rather than the positives? Do you say things like: "There's something wrong about that guy"; "She has a bad spirit"; or "They have issues, I can't tell you what—just pray for them"?

Criticism is the act of judging and finding fault; it's to blame or condemn for wrongdoing. A critical spirit has an obsession with what is flawed. It seeks to tear down, rather than build them up. It's a compulsion to focus on the negative, draw it out into the open, and make an issue of it.

Unfortunately, finding fault and being critical come naturally to our sinful, human nature. This is why Jesus warned us: "*Judge not, that you be not judged*" (Matthew 7:1). In other words, a judgmental attitude is dangerous, and He goes onto explain why: "*For with what judgment you judge, you will be judged; and with the measure you use, it will be measured back to you*" (Matthew 7:2). God, in His disdain for a critical spirit, will actually provoke others to mirror your attitude back onto you! He will raise up critical spirits around you to treat you as harshly as you have treated others. It's what happened to the governors and satraps: the lions' den, into which they threw Daniel, contained the same lions that devoured them.

It's one thing to recognize faults in others. It's another thing to make an issue of them. It's the difference between being healthy and unhealthy.

A healthy person can recognize what may be wrong in others, but understands he cannot righteously judge them because he cannot see into their hearts. Motives and intentions are more important than actions and performance. And, because they cannot know motives, healthy people leave the judgment and criticism to God. Unhealthy people, however, cannot control themselves. They have such a low opinion of themselves, everything they see is through a broken lens. Much of what they perceive is through the context of their own brokenness and they are compelled to focus on the negative.

If you want to go to the next level, you must put away a critical spirit. Stop throwing people to the lions. The same measure you use will be measured back to you. If you want to be surrounded by supportive, empowering, encouraging people who will promote you and move you higher, then be that kind of a person to others. Show patience, compassion, and understanding. Learn to give people "the benefit of the doubt" and see how those same blessings come back to you.

Do you have a gossipy tongue? Gossip is derogatory conversation about other people. It's repeating a bad report and often involves betraying a confidence, spreading personal information, and making disparaging judgments about another person. Gossip takes criticism to the next level. It broadcasts the flaws and failures of others with the effect of framing them in a negative context. It's malicious. Even if the gossiper doesn't believe he speaks with evil intent, if his negative report creates a negative perception in the hearer, then his words are poison and his influence is toxic.

The governors and satraps ran to the king with their information on Daniel. They couldn't wait to report his failure and diminish the king's opinion of him. In so doing, they hoped to elevate themselves. Ultimately, this is what gossip is about: It's an attempt to tear others down so the gossiper can feel better about himself while inflating his ego with a sense of importance. Gossip is like a narcotic. People who are insecure and have feelings of inadequacy will feel better when they talk about others in a derogatory manner, especially others who are successful or have achieved some level of popularity. The gossiper feels important because he has knowledge that no one else has obtained and can rouse people's interest. The effect is drug-like: just a few spiteful words, shared in confidence, can give frail egos a temporary boost.

Unfortunately, the only people that are impressed by the gossiper are governors and satraps—those who need to tear others down to elevate themselves. Don't make the mistake of thinking that throwing mud at others will boost your value. It won't. It just makes you muddy. In fact, it has the reverse affect with people of excellence. They see it for what it is—the attempt of a weak mind to prop itself up by tearing others down.

Nothing diminishes a person's worth more than a gossipy tongue. Smart people know that gossipers are low value individuals who cannot be trusted and reason, "Certainly, if a gossiper speaks badly about others, it's just a matter of time until they speak badly about me." This is why gossip betrays a weakness of character and a lack of integrity, and will always land in the lions' den.

Do you have an excuse to be mediocre? Too many people today have an attitude that rationalizes their inferiority, perpetuates their mediocrity, and even justifies it with theology. Poor performance has found a home in our modern-day, hyper-grace theology. We say, "God uses the foolish and weak, rather than the wise and mighty," and relax in the notion that God will use us even though our effort is poor. But that misses the point. God will make us effective by His Spirit and grace, but that can never be an excuse for a lack of excellence.

Ecclesiastes 9:10 says, "*Whatever your hand finds to do, do it with your might...*" and 2 Timothy 2:15 tells us, "*Be diligent to present yourself approved to God, a worker who does not need to be ashamed...*" This is not a theology that excuses mediocrity—it's a theology that denounces it. In Matthew 25, the Master gave talents to each of His servants. The servants who performed to the upper range of their talent and skill and produced a harvest were rewarded. The servant who underperformed was called wicked and lazy and was condemned to outer darkness.

Excellence isn't about being the best—it's about doing your best. Excellence is not about being the best singer, or the most successful in business, or preaching the greatest sermons ever heard. No, it's about doing the best we can do for the glory of God. Offering Him a substandard effort or anything less than our absolute best is no different than those Old Testament worshippers who offered God their blind and sick and expected Him to accept it. His response came through the prophet in Malachi 1:8-14:

> "*And when you offer the blind as a sacrifice, Is it not evil? And when you offer the lame and sick, Is it not evil? Offer it then to your governor! Would he be pleased with you? Would he accept you favorably? Says the LORD of hosts... 'But cursed be the deceiver Who has in his flock a male, but sacrifices to the Lord what is blemished—For I am a great King,' Says the LORD of hosts, 'And My name is to be feared among the nations.'*"

A Final Word

Ascending to the next level does not "just happen." Success is not egalitarian. Promotion is not an entitlement. It comes to those who excel—those who pay the price. The question you must answer for yourself is, "How much am I willing to pay in self-discipline, hard work, and personal sacrifice?"

The answer to this question is important because the cost is great. It means sacrificing immediate gratification for long term gain. It means putting away what is easy and comfortable and taking up what is hard and challenging. Excellence means casting aside your excuses and resisting the urge to blame those around you. Excellence is not a matter of gender, race, age, occupation, or even talent. It's about work ethic, appearance, and body language. It's about energy level, attitude, passion, teachability, and going the extra mile. It's about being prepared, being on time, and choosing healthy associates. If you're willing to accept these as your personal responsibilities, if you're willing to perform and prove your value rather than waiting for others to "make things happen," the sky will be your limit! You will soar like an eagle!

CHAPTER TWO

DILIGENCE

> **"** ***God can certainly move your mountain, but don't be surprised if He hands you a shovel.***

What would you say is your most valuable, personal asset? Which of your great qualities do you believe can take you to the "next level?" Perhaps it's a physical feature that enhances your appearance or a special talent that makes you shine. Or, maybe it's an ability to relate well to people or a charming, charismatic flare. While each of these may be important qualities, there is one virtue that outranks them all: diligence.

It's what scripture calls a "man's precious possession." The Hebrew word is "mâhîyr." It means to move quickly and do your best; to act with skillful haste. Diligence is about effort. It's about quality of work. Our English word for "diligence" is derived from the Latin "industria" which means to be steadfast in one's labors. Despite obstacles and difficulty, no matter what stands in their way, people with diligence will work tirelessly to achieve their goals and stay committed to the task regardless of cost or discomfort.

Obviously, gifting and skills are important. Proverbs 18:16 says, "*A man's gift makes room for him, and brings him before great men.*" It's true—if you have a special gift, there's often a place for you. If you can sing, someone will offer you a microphone. If you can preach, we'll give you a pulpit. Perhaps you can administrate or lead, then you'll find a title and be put to work. But while a man's gift may result in quick promotion or applause, such recognition will be short lived without the one, all-important quality of diligence. Your talent may get you in the "room" but it's diligence that will keep you there. Proverbs 12:25 says, "*the hand of the diligent will rule.*" In other words, diligence is what takes a person to the next level.

Every story of sustainable success involves a narrative of diligence. Perhaps one of the greatest examples is Nehemiah and the rebuilding of the wall of Jerusalem. From his account we discover several truths about next level living and the qualities of diligence that propel us higher.

Diligence Is Responsibility

"And it came to pass in the month of Nisan, in the twentieth year of King Artaxerxes, when wine was before him, that I took the wine and gave it to the king. Now I had never been sad in his presence before. Therefore the king said to me, 'Why is your face sad, since you are not sick? This is nothing but sorrow of heart.' So I became dreadfully afraid, and said to the king, 'May the king live forever! Why should my face not be sad, when the city, the place of my fathers' tombs, lies waste, and its gates are burned with fire?' Then the king said to me, 'What do you request?' So I prayed to the God of heaven. And I said to the king, 'If it pleases the king, and if your servant has found favor in your sight, I ask that you send me to Judah, to the city of my fathers' tombs, that I may rebuild it." - Nehemiah 2:1-5

Originally, he was a cupbearer to the king. It was a great job, taste-testing the king's delicacies, not only to ensure their worthiness of the king's noble palette, but also to protect the king from poisonous assassination attempts. But despite his comfy job, he could not escape the burden he had for his homeland. Jerusalem had never recovered from the Babylonian invasion almost a century before. What was left of the city remained in ruins and his beloved people were prey to their surrounding enemies.

Rather than turn a deaf ear and say, "It's not my job," Nehemiah took responsibility and, like David, would cry, "Is there not a cause?" He felt a burden to take action, to get involved, to do something. And if he did not, he would convict himself with private shame for having done nothing. This is the birthing room of diligence—a sense of responsibility.

Responsibility is taking ownership of expectations and demands that are assigned, assumed or imposed upon us and morally obligating ourselves to the consequences of whether or not we have fulfilled those demands. The diligent person accepts the burden of "doing what he can," not because he is being paid or because he will suffer if he doesn't, but simply because it's his moral obligation to so. This is what drives diligence. It's a continuous awareness that "it's up to me to make a difference and if I don't act, part of the blame must fall to me." Hence, the diligent take initiative; they are self-starters and hard workers. They are not dependent on someone else's motivation; they are motivated by a self-imposed ethical obligation.

Diligence Is a Sense of Duty

"*Then I said to them, 'You see the distress that we are in, how Jerusalem lies waste, and its gates are burned with fire. Come and let us build the wall of Jerusalem, that we may no longer be a reproach.' And I told them of the hand of my God which had been good upon me, and also of the king's words that he had spoken to me. So they said, 'Let us rise up and build.' Then they set their hands to this good work.*" - Nehemiah 2:17-18

Diligence is more than hard work; it's hard work that rises from loyalty to a cause. It's a unique kind of commitment that surpasses one's loyalty to serve his or her own private interests or personal convenience.

Consider those who serve in the military, law enforcement, or as first responders. Their vocation requires them to put their lives on the line in service to others. Every day they put the cause before themselves, their ambitions, and even their families. Sociologists call it an "Institutional Mindset." It's a mentality that places the needs of the society, the group, or the organization as a priority over one's personal needs. First responders do it every day, faithfully and selflessly, and, as a result, we call them heroes—and they are.

This is the essence of duty—it's a loyalty to the cause. And those who share it have a different mentality than most people today, especially those of us in civilian life. We don't have an institutional mindset. We don't have a primary commitment to a society or organization—our primary commitment is to ourselves. This is why most people, when faced with a certain level of sacrifice or self-denial, will find themselves asking, "What's in it for me? What am I getting out of this?" As a result, their quality of work will diminish—as will their commitment—until they finally justify their lack of diligence and find an excuse to quit.

By contrast, the man or woman of diligence will go on because they are driven by something deeper. They are driven by a sense of honor—an inner need to do what is right, not for themselves, but for the institution they serve.

Nehemiah had this sense of duty. He had a mindset that elevated the needs of Israel above his own needs. He said, "*See the distress that we are in, how Jerusalem lies waste, and its gates are burned with fire. Come and let us build the wall of Jerusalem, that we may no longer be a reproach.*" It was a sense of duty: a commitment to a cause greater than himself.

In a speech to the U.S. Naval Academy, David Brooks said, "Too often we hear preachers, motivational gurus, and university commencement speakers tell their audiences: 'Find your passion. Look inside to see what you love. Know what your passion is and make your life about that.' That is really bad advice—unless we're trying to build a culture of narcissists whose primary concern is 'What makes me happy?' People of character don't look inside for a passion, they look outside at the world and see what problems need solving and make their lives about that. They ask, 'What are the world's greatest needs and how can my abilities and aptitudes meet those needs?' Their passion, their duty, is not determined by what life can give to them, it's determined by what life is calling them to do."[1]

Though they exist, diligent people are becoming harder to find. Most people commit to a task only to that level of their own comfort and self-interest. They have little tolerance for duty—especially the kind of duty that requires them to deny personal needs and preferences. Paradoxically, this is also why diligence is the great distinguisher. Nothing gives you more distinction and differentiates you from the crowd like diligence. Like no other virtue, diligence is a launch pad for promotion. In fact, one cannot rise to the "next level" without it. This is why Proverbs 22:29 tells us diligence causes one to "*stand before kings and not unknown men.*" Those who are building great organizations understand the value of duty and diligence, and they will regard those with such character among their most valued assets.

Diligence Is Work Ethic

"*So we rebuilt the wall till all of it reached half its height, for the people worked with all their heart.*" - Nehemiah 4:6

Diligence is work ethic—it's the moral obligation to do one's best. It means you don't look for an easy way out or leave the difficult jobs for someone else. If something needs be fixed, you fix it. If something needs to be cleaned, you clean it. If something must be done, you do it. It's this demonstration of character that distinguishes you as a person of value, deserving of promotion and advance.

Success doesn't "just happen." It happens because diligence made it happen. Lou Holtz, the only college football coach to lead six different college football programs to bowl games and four different programs to the final top 20 rankings, understood the value of diligence. He said, "Winners embrace hard work. They love the discipline of it, the trade-off they're making to win. Losers, on the other hand, see it as punishment. And that's the difference."

Diligence isn't suffering, it's the fertile soil of opportunity. It's the difference between winning and losing, success and failure, and going to the next level or staying stuck in complacency. Opportunity is not sitting idle and waiting for someone to open a door for you. Opportunity is found in the hustle and hard work. It's early mornings and late nights. It's long, hot days and tired afternoons. Opportunity presents itself in the refusal to cut corners and quit. Opportunity doesn't just appear—it's provoked, incited, and inspired to appear by diligence. Work hard—harder than anyone else—and see how opportunity presents itself. Thomas Edison said, "Opportunity is missed by most people because it's dressed in overalls and looks like work."

This is especially important for people of faith to understand. It's amazing how many Christians believe success will come if they simply get a "man of God" to lay hands on them or a "prophet" to prophesy over them. They believe the con-artist-preachers who say, "Bring an offering and I'll pray an anointing upon your life for success and prosperity." Or, "Come to my church and I'll lay hands on you and impart an unction for favor in your business." New cars, new homes, more clients, greater revenue—all you need is a prayer or an anointing. I even heard one preacher toting his "Holy-Ghost-Anointed Pens." He said, "Use these pens that are anointed by God and you'll pass every exam and succeed in every contract you sign."

Nonsense. Not only is it unbiblical, it's a heresy that borders on witchcraft. It's spiritual junk food. It has no nutritional value or substance. There's no talk of hard work, discipline, study, preparation, core competencies, or simply having a good attitude. Just get someone to pray for you and you will succeed. Ludicrous. If there is any formula for success or prescription for promotion, it's not found in a prophet's prayer—it's found in diligence.

In Matthew 25, Jesus emphasized the need for diligence in His Parable of the Talents. There were three workers. Each was given resources according to his ability. One was given five talents, another two talents, and the last was given one talent. The reward they received, the next level to which each was assigned, was proportionate to their performance—their diligence. Those who worked hard, properly prepared, demonstrated diligence, and became productive were promoted. Those who did not were condemned.

The message is clear. God has incredible plans for our lives. There are things He wants to release to us, there are blessings He wants to give us, but the key to receiving them is diligence. This is what He meant when Jesus said, "*Well done, good and faithful servant; you have been faithful over a few things, I will make you ruler over many things.*" There's no mention of one's special gifting, talent, or skill. Those who worked hard—who demonstrated diligence—where promoted to the next level.

Diligence Is Time Management

"*So we labored in the work, and half of the men held the spears from daybreak until the stars appeared. At the same time I also said to the people, 'Let each man and his servant stay at night in Jerusalem, that they may be our guard by night and a working party by day.' So neither I, my brethren, my servants, nor the men of the guard who followed me took off our clothes, except that everyone took them off for washing.*" - Nehemiah 4:21-23

There is no diligence without the effective use of one's time. To be accurate, there is no such thing as "managing time." No one can manage time. We all have the same 168 hours in a week and no one has ever learned how to slow time, increase time, or manage time. It's actually about "managing yourself" in relation to the limited time you have. The following are a few practical techniques that diligent people use.

Use a calendar. Having a calendar is the most fundamental step to managing your daily activities. Proper management of time begins with a centralized matrix that organizes important events, meetings, and deadlines

Know your deadlines. When do you need to finish your tasks? Mark the deadlines out clearly in your calendar or organizer so you know when you need to finish them. If possible, set reminders to keep you on track.

Use project schedules. Also known as Gantt charts or promotion schedules, these organize essential tasks in relation to completion deadlines. More specifically, they illustrate the start and finish dates of the terminal elements and summarize those elements of a project.

Have an organized workspace. If you have a messy workspace, you will feel disorganized and sluggish. You won't even feel like doing anything since it's so disorganized. By contrast, if you have a tidy and organized workspace, you'll be inspired to get work done. You can find your things easily rather than waste precious minutes sieving through your pile of papers for something you need but cannot find.

Create a weekly plan. The first thing you do on the first morning of your work week (or the last morning of the previous week), review the week to come and identify main priorities and tasks that need to be completed. As an added step, allocate blocks of time throughout the week to focus on certain items.

Create a daily plan. Plan your day before it unfolds. Do it in the morning or, even better, toward the end of the previous day. This plan gives you a good overview of how the day will pan out.

Know your top three priorities every day. This includes meetings to be had, people to call, problems to confront, and tasks to complete.

Prioritize with a check list. Whether it's the weekly plan or the daily plan, checklists are vital. Put first things first and keep the most important items at the top of the list. There are a million different things we can pick to do. Some will be important things that make a difference and the rest will be unimportant things that actually don't make any difference at all. Out of these many tasks, we must pick and choose, otherwise we will drown in seemingly endless tasks and never get anything done. Focus on the important and deprioritize the latter.

Focus on one thing at a time. Most of us can do one thing well at a time. The more you try to multitask, the more likely the quality of work will diminish with each of those tasks. It may feel like you're saving time, but in reality, because you're likely to miss crucial elements or miss things entirely, you'll waste more time making necessary corrections.

Be firm with your time, but be flexible. Be careful not to view people and their needs as interruptions to your work; if you're a leader, they *are* your work. These are your team members who need to hear from you. They need your feedback. They need your encouragement. It's recommended that you schedule regular time with essential team members to control interruptions while at the same time giving them the access they need.

Eliminate your time wasters. There are things that steal time: Facebook and other social networks are the most common. As are email, phone calls, and excessive texting.

Block out other distractions like Facebook and other forms of social media unless you use these tools to generate business. In reality, you should not be updating your social networks while on work time—that is the same as stealing.

Delay answering the phone when possible. Just because your phone is ringing doesn't mean you have to answer it now—unless that is your job portfolio. Instead, post a voicemail saying you'll call back by a certain time and schedule an hour to return your phone calls. Be careful with this—always remember that there are some people that should always have access to you, such as your "up-line" personnel (bosses, management, executives, etc.).

Many times, a voice is better than an email. Obviously, there are times when it's better to use email because you want to memorialize directions or make sure things are properly communicated. However, many times it's better to pick up the phone or walk down the hall and talk directly to colleagues. You can give precise direction and clear up misunderstandings quickly. This also helps to avoid future wasted time because of miscommunication, or offense.

Cut off conversations when necessary. Learn how to exit meetings and conversations that are taking too much time. Don't be afraid to interrupt the meeting or draw a line to cut-off. This is usually most effective when announced at the beginning of an exchange. You can say, "I have a hard stop at 2:00 P.M." Or if a phone call is too long, "I'm gonna have to let you go." Then, there is always the very considerate, "I don't want to use up any more of your time."

Learn to say "no." This is one of the most important, and often the most difficult. We don't want to hurt someone's feelings or let them down, so we don't say "no" to their requests. However, we must remember, every time we say "yes" to one thing, we are saying "no" to something or someone else. Here are some suggestions on how to say "no."

First, acknowledge the request by stating: "I understand the boss has put a lot on you lately and you're under deadlines."

Second, decline briefly: "That won't work for me right now, but I'll get back to you if anything changes." Or, "I really appreciate you thinking of me, but I've just got too much on my plate right now."

Third, give a non-specific reason for your "no" but keep it vague so they don't argue with your reason or try to change your mind. Tell them: "I have a family commitment I cannot change." (Of course, people don't need to know that your commitment is dinner at home with your family or going to your son's football game.)

Fourth, generate options. Rather than leaving the person hanging, offer another option that is more suitable to you. Tell them: "Here's what I can do for you. I can come in early tomorrow or work through lunch Wednesday." Or, "I can try to get someone else to help you." Or, "I can work today until 5:30 P.M."

Learn to delegate. Is there someone else who can do it? Perhaps it may not be done as well as you can do it, or exactly as you would like it to be done. But ask yourself the question, "Does it really have to be done exactly the way I would do it? Or would the way someone else will do it be good enough?"

Be mindful of manipulators. There are actual persuasion techniques that people often use when making an "ask." Beware of these when protecting your time.

Reciprocity. People often give you something before making an "ask." This is because they know about the psychological tendency to want to reciprocate.

Making two "asks." When people ask for something and you say no, they increase the odds that when they ask for something else (usually something smaller), you'll say yes. "Well, if you won't donate $100, could you at least help us out with $50?"

Anchoring. "Most people donate $100." Or, "Everyone else volunteered an evening during the week." This is an attempt to obligate you to a certain expectation that they have projected.

Guilt. Some askers will remind you of how many times you've said "no" in the past, or how many others have given their time.

Physical attractiveness. Yes, it's true. There are those who try to manipulate you by flaunting certain physical features. Realize, it's not you they are attracted to, it's what you can do for them.

Diligence Is Strategic

"So it was, from that time on, that half of my servants worked at construction, while the other half held the spears, the shields, the bows, and wore armor; and the leaders were behind all the house of Judah. Those who built on the wall, and those who carried burdens, loaded themselves so that with one hand they worked at construction, and with the other held a weapon. Every one of the builders had his sword girded at his side as he built. And the one who sounded the trumpet was beside me." - Nehemiah 4:16-18

The famous inventor and entrepreneur Thomas Edison said, "Vision without execution is hallucination." From the phonograph to the light bulb to the motion picture to his 1,093 patents, Edison's inventions changed the world. But the man also failed, sometimes enormously. In response to a question about his many blunders, Edison said, "I have not failed 10,000 times, I've successfully found 10,000 ways that will not work."

This is the difference between those who dream about the next level and those who actually get there. When Edison had a vision, he didn't dream about it, he did it! Sure, he failed—sometimes huge. But what he didn't do is have empty dreams that never accomplished anything.

The world is full of dreamers who aspire to achieve. However, most of them never get off the ground because they fail to take the practical steps to get them there. Edison would say they are hallucinating because they never converted the dream to an actionable reality that could be systematically executed.

Successful people know that merely talking and dreaming does not advance one's promotion, nor does it bring measurable results that can be achieved. However, having a strategy for achieving one's next level drives you to execute on that vision.

Proverbs 14:15 tells us, "*The prudent considers well his steps*." In other words, it's the wise person that is forward thinking, forward planning and forward moving. Proverbs 24:3-5 further states: "*Through wisdom a house is built, and by understanding it is established; by knowledge the rooms are filled with all precious and pleasant riches. A wise man is strong, yes, a man of knowledge increases strength; for by wise counsel you will wage your own war, and in a multitude of counselors there is safety.*"

It's an exhortation about strategic planning. Moses, Joshua, David, Nehemiah, Paul the Apostle, and even Jesus, were all strategic. They did not merely dream, they converted dreams to actionable realities and executed on them. This is what diligent people do: they project their assent to the next level, plan their steps accordingly and take action, being careful to evaluate and measure their progress along the way.

Strategy requires vision. Vision is the ability to see a reality that does not yet exist. It's a firm conviction of where one is going—a vivid idea of what the future should hold, including the passion to achieve it and the ability to communicate it. No one ever achieved the next level without first having a vision of what that level looked like.

Strategy admits the brutal facts. Diligent people are honest regarding their current reality. They don't try to make things appear better than they are. They admit their failures and acknowledge their deficiencies. It's an essential part of the journey. How can one effectively move forward in a sustainable way without recognizing where they have fallen short and which corrections must be made? They cannot. And diligence ensures that the brutal facts are addressed.

Strategy identifies work plans. Every strategy requires goals. These are the key target areas of improvement—the systematic steps that must be taken to ensure progress. Goals answer the question, "What targets must be achieved in order to get to the next level?" Moreover, work plans drill down and ask, "What objectives must be attained that are essential in achieving those targets?" Each step is reduced to a series of preceding steps which become the mile markers on the road map to success.

Strategy delegates and assigns resources. Diligent people don't sit idly waiting for others to figure things out. They have the ability to connect the dots. They recognize what resources are needed, which people are capable, and how the work should flow. Diligence takes the lead, it makes things happen, it challenges inaction, and organizes people and resources into processes that execute.

Strategy measures progress. If a goal is not measurable, it's not attainable. There must be metrics in place to evaluate if the strategy is working. Diligent people understand timelines and deadlines and are willing to hold people accountable. They know that no one floats into success—the next level is an uphill journey that requires the constant progress of push and pull.

Strategy is financially sound. Every vision has a price tag. There will be costs and diligent people take the extra step of considering costs involved. Even Jesus said the wise builder will first, "*sit down and count the cost*" before beginning his project (Luke 14:28). It's been said that budget should never determine vision. While that seems like faith, it oversteps a certain reality: How you budget determines if you will achieve your vision. "Counting the cost" is not a sign that a person is doubting—it may be a sign that a person is thinking.

Obviously, work plans, organizational management, and budgeting are not sexy. Most people just want to have an exciting event, launch a missions project, or conduct a sensational, world-shaking miracle rally in the middle of the city. That sounds great, but for every missions project, every successful event, and every miracle crusade, there are people, behind the scenes, executing a strategy. It's called "Due Diligence." They are planning, recruiting, organizing, coordinating, and evaluating. Success doesn't "just happen." It happens because diligence made it happen.

Diligence Is a Good Attitude

"*Now it happened, when Sanballat, Tobiah, the Arabs, the Ammonites, and the Ashdodites heard that the walls of Jerusalem were being restored and the gaps were beginning to be closed, that they became very angry, and all of them conspired together to come and attack Jerusalem and create confusion. Nevertheless we made our prayer to our God, and because of them we set a watch against them day and night.*" - Nehemiah

4:7-9

Attitudes are contagious and bad attitudes are more contagious than good ones. It's easy to catch sickness from someone who is ill, but it's nearly impossible to catch health from someone who is healthy. Bad attitudes are toxic and can destroy an organization. Good attitudes are essential and must be deliberately demonstrated by those who desire the next level.

Nehemiah reminds us that there will always be resistance. No matter how noble our vision or honorable our work ethic, obstacles will come to prevent our progress. Through it all, however, Nehemiah never compromised his attitude. He responded to hardship with faith. He prayed, believed, and remained optimistic that God would bring them success.

Diligent people understand the power of attitude and they work hard to have a good one. Zig Ziglar said: "Attitude, not aptitude, determines altitude." It determines how far you will go or how quickly you will stop. If you're going to achieve the next level, the attitude you have at your current level will decide if you go higher.

Chuck Swindol, former president of the Dallas Theological Seminary, said, "Life is ten percent what happens to me and ninety percent how I react to it." And how we react determines what doors will open and what doors remain shut. Swindol went on to say:

> "*The longer I live, the more I realize the impact of attitude on life. Attitude, to me, is more important than facts. It is more important than the past, than education, than money, than circumstances, than failures, than successes, than what other people think or say or do. It is more important than appearance, giftedness, or skill. It will make or break a company, a church, a home. The remarkable thing is we have a choice every day regarding the attitude we will embrace for that day.*"

No one can change their past. No one can control the future. No one can make people do what they want them to do. But there is a power you have that can turn your past into testimony, your future into a destiny, and pull people around you in unity. Attitude is the greatest power a person has.

In 1 Samuel 22, David was living in the Cave of Adullam. The Bible says "*...everyone who was in distress, everyone who was in debt, and everyone who was discontented gathered to him. So he became captain over them. And there were about four hundred men with him.*" Why did four hundred men gather to David? He had no great vision, no wealth, power, or privilege. David was a fugitive from the law, branded by King Saul as a traitor and living in a cave. But despite all that, people flocked to him and wanted to follow him. Why? Because there was something about that man—something in his spirit, something in his attitude—that people could not resist.

Perhaps it was the way he kept singing those psalms of praise in the back of the cave. Regardless of how bad things would get, David never despaired. He could be heard on his harp, late into the night, his sweet voice raised in worship to his God, singing: "*The Lord is my shepherd; I shall not want.*"

They came to him, by the hundreds, because of his spirit—the way he inspired those who followed him. His attitude was encouraging, uplifting, and life-giving. John Maxwell wrote: "Many people who approach the area of vision in leadership have it all backward. They believe that if the cause is good enough, people will automatically buy into it and follow. But that's not how leadership really works. People don't at first follow worthy causes. They follow worthy leaders who promote worthwhile causes. People buy into the leader first, then the leader's vision."

People today have enough discouragement and despair in their life. They don't want to be around someone who is always complaining and resentful toward circumstances. If you're a grump—always negative and condescending—people will not want to be around you. You will be destined for smallness. But if you can lift people's spirits with hope and optimism—if you can energize people, make them laugh, make them thankful, make them feel good about themselves, their lives, and their potential—then they will always want to be around you and push you higher.

If you increase attitude, you increase your value. If you increase your value, you increase your opportunity. Diligent people are aware of their attitude and how they rate in the organization. Where do you rate?

The Common Commodity: This is the average worker who shows up when expected and leaves at the exact end of the day. They do no more than anyone else and no less than what is expected.

The Increasing Asset: This person looks at every project with the mindset, "How can I make this better. What can I do to go the extra mile and distinguish myself?" They are willing to do the jobs other people avoid. They get their hands dirty and go above and beyond the call of duty.

The Morale Booster: There are many people who are talented and do their job well. They even go the extra mile and show competent skills. Unfortunately, some of these same people are difficult to work with; they are abrasive and unkind. These people, despite their efficient skills, cap their value in the workplace. By contrast, those with competent skills who can also work well with others are highly valued. Their morale, unifying attitude and camaraderie will positively effect the culture and generate good attitudes in others. These people are usually the first to be promoted in the workplace.

The Problem Solver: This is where one's potential value begins to be revealed. The problem solver is solutions oriented. Her approach is not to say, "There is a problem that management needs to resolve." Rather, she says, "We have a problem and here are three solutions that could fix it. Which one do you want me to implement?" Managers love this approach. This is how diligent people approach problems. They take responsibility, even if the problem isn't theirs. They offer solutions, not just challenges. And in doing so, they demonstrate incredible value to the organization.

The Indispensable Influence: People of this caliber are actively engaged in the success of the organization. They contribute to the vision and direction of the company. They proactively identify issues and find ways to implement solutions. They save money, they increase efficiency, they promote productivity, and move the organization closer to its goals. This is the highest level of diligence—the attitude that demonstrates its high value by the real time impact it's having.

Diligence Is Consistency

"*Then Eliashib the high priest rose up with his brethren the priests and built the Sheep Gate; they consecrated it and hung its doors. They built as far as the Tower of the Hundred, and consecrated it, then as far as the Tower of Hananel.*" - Nehemiah 3:1

Almost everyone likes to think they are diligent, but diligence is not true until it's been tested.

The test does not come in the accomplishment of some grand feat done in the spotlight. Rather, diligence is tested in the mundane. True diligence is revealed in the everyday, ordinary, non-glamorous execution of menial tasks. When no one is watching or no one cares—when you're tired, bored, and wearied by the dull routine of the monotonous—that's where one's work ethic is truly revealed.

In Chapter 3, Nehemiah lists the many people who were essential to the building of the wall. No one person was more important than another. No one is noted for some grand, spectacular feat which made him or her famous. Rather, each one is recognized for the menial, mundane tasks that they did with consistent excellence. Herein lies the true nature of diligence: the discipline to remain consistent—even when consistent is boring, unglamorous, and obscure.

Professional basketball icon Julius Erving said, "Being a professional is doing the things you know to do, on the days you don't feel like doing them." There will always be "those days" and how you perform at that time, reveals your diligence.

What drives a person to the next level is not accomplishing some great act, it's consistency in the little acts. It's returning to your assignment day after day, night after night, with the same level of effort and the same work ethic, without loss of enthusiasm or commitment to excellence. Helen Keller, a woman born blind and deaf, who rose to distinction in the 19th century having become the first blind and deaf person to earn a bachelor of arts degree said, "I long to accomplish some great and noble task, but it's my chief duty to accomplish small tasks as if they were great and noble." Beryl Markham, the first female pilot to fly solo across the Atlantic Ocean from east to west said, "If a man has any greatness in him, it comes to light, not in one flamboyant hour, but in the ledger of his daily work."

Any singer can sing one or two great songs. Any preacher can preach three or four great sermons. Any salesman can make a half dozen great sales. Even a broken clock looks great twice a day. But true greatness, true distinction, is demonstrating a standard of consistent diligence throughout the day, not merely once or twice when you're in the spotlight.

There is an important lesson about this in the story of Joshua and his march around Jericho. In that event, we tend to focus mostly on the miracle of the last day, when the walls collapsed. It's an incredible miracle, but not the main point of the story. The real story is "the march" and what happened in the seven days before the victory.

It must have seemed like a ridiculous strategy—at least from the perspective of the soldiers. For them, battle was easy: overwhelm the enemy with brute force and fight until you drop. But that wasn't God's plan. He told Joshua to march the people around the city, once every day for six days and seven times on the seventh day. There was to be no talking, no singing, not noise at all—not a sound during those marches. On the final march of the last day, however, they were to shout and blow their trumpets. One can imagine all Joshua's mighty, battle hardened warriors shaking their heads sarcastically: "Wow, that's a winning strategy."

But what they needed to learn was that the key factor in victory is "how we march." Yes, victory ultimately comes through God's miraculous provision, but our obedience and consistent diligence is a part of the process. In fact, it's through the march—the effort we put forth—that we learn and grow, and qualify ourselves for the next level.

In the march, the key was consistency. They had to repeat the routine every day, even though there was no change in the circumstance, no difference in the wall. The first day, no cracks developed—but still they marched. The second day, no tremors in the ground—but still they marched. The third and fourth day, the walls stood strong—but still they marched. The fifth day, the sixth day, nothing, no change, not even a brick came loose—but still they marched. And then came the seventh day: the first march, the second march, the third, fourth, fifth, sixth—each time they went through the same routine, the same attention to detail, the same march—but nothing changed. Then came the seventh march on the seventh day. Imagine the ridicule coming from inside the walls, the laughter from the Jerichoites. They probably threw stones from atop the wall, along with rotting garbage, and hurled insults at the horde of silent, marching Israelites.

Imagine the army, for seven days they followed Joshua but nothing changed. Some were probably getting ready to turn against him—maybe soldiers in the army, their uniforms stained from rotten tomatoes, were about to mutiny. But Joshua remained resolute—just as steadfast and consistent on the last march as he was on the first. He had firm attention to detail, making sure he marched exactly as God commanded. His demeanor never changed. His confidence never wavered. He had the same enthusiasm, the same pace, and the same determination. He was the picture of resolve, demonstrated by a diligent commitment to follow through on exactly what God told him to do.

Sure, we know the walls came down, but that's not the point. It was the march that made the difference in Joshua's life. It was the march that taught Joshua about faith and trust and how God works. It was the march that showed him how to hear the voice of God. It was the march that taught him about leadership and humility, consistency and diligence, authority and obedience. It was the march that distinguished Joshua as a leader with credibility equal to that of Moses. It was the march that made him great and legendary. There is value in the march.

The next level does not come through miracles. There is no such thing as an instant breakthrough or an overnight success. Joshua teaches us there has to be a march—a season of patiently enduring and being diligent and consistent and obedient even when nothing seems to change. There must be a resolve to continue, a determination to move forward and work hard, to upgrade your competency, to keep a good attitude, to manage your time, to think strategically, and to resist laziness. This is the march and Joshua teaches us that if we will keep marching, there will be a breakthrough. If we stay diligent, there will be success. It may not be overnight. In fact, it won't be overnight. But the next level will come. And with it comes wisdom, experience, character, and credibility.

There is value in the march.

Diligence Overcomes Procrastination

"Now it happened when Sanballat, Tobiah, Geshem the Arab, and the rest of our enemies heard that I had rebuilt the wall, and that there were no breaks left in it (though at that time I had not hung the doors in the gates), that Sanballat and Geshem sent to me, saying, 'Come, let us meet together among the villages in the plain of Ono.' But they thought to do me harm. So I sent messengers to them, saying, 'I am doing a great work, so that I cannot come down. Why should the work cease while I leave it and go down to you?'" - Nehemiah 6:1-3

When the enemy realizes he can't stop you, he'll settle for distracting you.

Nehemiah's enemies knew it was futile to make him quit, so they simply tried to slow him down. "Come, let us meet together," they said. It was an attempt to distract him from his work by putting his focus on something else. Fortunately, Nehemiah was discerning of the enemy's tactics and rebuked their invitation to procrastinate: "I am doing a great work. Why should the work cease while I leave it and go down to you?" He recognized the conspiracy. His adversaries intended, not merely to slow him down, but to use distraction and procrastination as a means to his demise.

Procrastination is not quitting outright. It's delaying, postponing, putting the project off until later. It's the "non-action" of avoiding certain kinds of unpleasant tasks in preference of more pleasurable ones. For those pursuing the next level, procrastination is professional suicide—it's the slow death of success.

No one is beyond the tendency to procrastinate. A recent article in *Psychology Today* reported that 20 percent of people admit to chronically avoiding difficult tasks and deliberately looking for distractions—which, unfortunately, are increasingly available in today's culture.[2] I think the other 80 percent are in denial.

Unfortunately, as common as procrastination is, it's the number one reason so many never make it to the next level. What are your dreams? What plans and goals do you see for your future. Sadly, many who have wonderful plans never do one thing to achieve them. Or, if they did start, they never finished because somewhere along the way, Sanballat and Geshem called to them from the valley of procrastination, and the worked ceased. Now, years later, the walls still are not repaired and their pursuit of the next level has become a forgotten dream. Procrastination is toxic.

If you don't believe how dangerous procrastinating is, interview some people in their sixties and seventies. Ask them of their regrets. Ask them if they wish they had done more with their lives when they had the chance. Ask them if they had their time again, what they would do differently. You will find that most of their regrets are not from evil works committed, but of good works omitted. The greatest regrets are for what they failed to do when it was in their power to do it. Procrastination is a thief.

The good news is if you're reading this, you're alive, and because you're alive, you still have the opportunity to achieve great things. But the first enemy to conquer is procrastination.

First, admit you're a procrastinator. Admit it. Confess it. But be realistic, don't sugarcoat it. Procrastination is laziness and if you admit to being a procrastinator, you admit to a problem with laziness. Laziness is a disinclination toward work or any task that is difficult, unpleasant, or uncomfortable. Tell yourself, "Stop being lazy." When you catch yourself procrastinating, deliver a rebuke, "You're being lazy again. Don't miss out on this opportunity to excel."

Second, understand the issue of motivation. Simply stated, we don't want to do something simply because we are not motivated to do it. Sounds simple, but it can actually be somewhat complex. When you understand what is driving or preventing you, it will be easier to overcome.

For some, they are distracted by immediate gratification. More specifically, they are unable to pursue tasks that bring long-term benefits because they are encumbered by what is attractive and feels good right now. It could be a social network update or an email, it could be phone call to a friend or cuddling with a favorite pet, it could be a nap or simply daydreaming. Whatever your distraction is, identify it as a pitfall to success and treat it as the adversary it is. Tell Sanballat and Geshem, "I'm not coming down to you until the work is done."

For others, the issue goes deeper. It could be a fear of failure or certain unpleasant emotional associations that accompany the performance of a task. In such cases, remember that these threats are ethereal—they are not real. Remind yourself that the greater threat is doing nothing and forfeiting your current opportunities.

Third, be proactive. Don't wait for procrastination to appear before you deal with it. What are those tasks you struggle with? When do you procrastinate? Determine to act before those circumstances arise and outline, in your mind, a plan of attack. Take control of your mind, your life. Don't be passive. Have a plan—decide your behavior before you get there —and act!

Fourth, get specific. Grab a pen and paper, and make a list of all the things you desire in your life. Doesn't matter how big or small the ambition. List every one of them down and identify the incremental steps you need to take to get you there. Check them off as you complete them or highlight them if you procrastinate. This is a form of accountability and it helps to build positive momentum in your life.

Fifth, celebrate the small things. Don't set your goals too high. Give yourself targets that are achievable and when you perform well, thank God and thank yourself! Tell somebody who will appreciate the small successes. You could even congratulate yourself with a special indulgence like extra time on your social network or taking your dog for a walk—what gives you enjoyment. Celebrate your victories.

Sixth, don't be discouraged. You may never completely overcome procrastination. There may always be areas where this struggle is present. Be honest with your failures, but give yourself some grace. It's about building momentum. If you're procrastinating, you have developed some bad habits, and reinforcing your success helps you to break them gradually.

CHAPTER THREE

COMPETENCE

> “ ***Don't be a typewriter person in a laptop world. By failing to upgrade, we make ourselves obsolete.***

It has often been said that God promotes a person to the level of their own incompetence. In other words, God sometimes elevates people who are not sufficiently prepared in order to demonstrate His strength through their weakness.

While this does happen, it's the exception, not the rule. More typically, preparation is essential to promotion. Moses endured 40 years of preparation in the backside of the desert, and Joshua was prepared for another 40 years as his protégé. Samuel had his school of the prophets and Jesus had a three-year school for His disciples. Paul spent an unknown number of years in the Arabian desert and told his apprentice Timothy that "*the man of God (should) be competent, equipped for every good work*" (2 Timothy 3:17, ESV). In other words, anointing is not enough—the call of God is not enough. One must acquire a certain level of competency to qualify for the next level.

Competence is having sufficient ability to do the job. It's a combination of spiritual gifts, personal values, and practical skills that enable an individual to perform a given task to successful standards. Competence is the key that unlocks opportunity—without it, opportunity will be lost. In other words, when the occasion for promotion is presented, those who have achieved certain abilities will enter in. Those who don't will be left behind.

God's Grace and Our Cooperation

There are two factors that are essential in the development of greater competency: God's grace and our cooperation.

On the one side is a gracious God who is "*working in us, both to will and to do for His good pleasure*" (Philippians 2:13). Scripture says, "*His divine power has given to us all things that pertain unto life and godliness*" (2 Peter 1:3), and, "*He faithful to complete that good work that He began in us*" (Philippians 1:6). God's call upon us is an "*upward call*" in Christ Jesus (Philippians 3:14) and He desires to take us to the next level.

On the other side is us. Although God wants to deepen our competency and qualify us for the next level, it requires our cooperation. Our participation with his working in us is the vital step in the process of our enlargement. Unfortunately, our attention is too often focused on our current level of comfort rather than the next level to which God is trying to bring us. This makes it difficult—if not impossible—to be confronted with low level attitudes that are holding us back.

People who increase their competency and qualify for the next level are able to hear and accept the bad news—about themselves. They can hear the brutal facts about their own character deficiencies and faulty performance and own it. In other words, they don't make excuses, shift the blame to others, or justify themselves. They acknowledge the need for changes to be made and set out to make them.

This dispels the notion that going to the next level is a fun-filled, magical journey for the one who simply desires it. No. Going to the next level is hard work. It's uncomfortable and painful. It forces us to confront ourselves and answer many difficult questions, beginning with the following three.

Question #1: Do I have deficiencies that hold me back?

Several years ago I was called to an urgent visit to an elderly parishioner in the hospital. After my visit ended and upon departure from the emergency room, I was struck by the distant cries of young girl down the hallway. Venturing closer, I could hear her pleas more distinctly: "No mama no! Make him stop, mama! It hurts, he's hurting me mama, make him stop!" Looking beyond the partially opened curtain, I could see a small girl being held down by her mother as a doctor was working on her leg. There was a deep gash in her calf and he was trying to stop the bleeding.

Her cries continued. Although, it seemed heartless and cruel, both the doctor and her mother knew that the little girl must submit to the painful procedure she was being forced to endure. The bleeding had to be stopped. The wound had to be cleaned. The tissue had to be sewn. If not, that little girl would forever be wounded and perhaps even crippled. The doctor, in his wisdom, forced that child to submit because he knew how crucial this procedure was to her future. He knew she was created to walk and run and leap and play. If she was to achieve all she had been created to achieve, she had to submit to the corrective process—no matter how painful.

It's a scenario often repeated by the Great Physician as He prepares us for our next level.

We'll call him Andrew. He was, by far, the most talented guitar player and musician I had ever met. His musical skill on the worship team brought every other musician to a higher level. It was apparent that he was meant for great heights in the kingdom of God. Unfortunately, Andrew had an issue. He was probably the meanest, orneriest person ever to step foot in our church.

Because of Andrew's musical expertise, he would often coach people privately. Unfortunately, because of his abrasive demeanor, he would leave his students offended, hurt, and terribly discouraged. I told Andrew that he needed to step down from his position until he learned how to be more patient and loving with people. I offered to meet with him and help develop his coaching skills. Sadly, Andrew rejected my counsel and left the church.

As he left, I told him that God had great plans for him, but he would never make it to the next level with his current demeanor. I told him that his bad attitude would be like a brass ceiling, always hindering him, no matter where he went and how many promotions he received. I told him this flaw in his character would always pull him back down—and it did. Andrew went from church to church to church, never able to achieve the heights that God intended.

And then there was Mary. Mary believed she had a specific call to the body of Christ. She claimed to be a prophet—according to her, like John the Baptist. While it was true that she had a prophetic gifting, and God had given her unique insights for the body of Christ, I told her she was no John the Baptist. In fact, I told her that for her to put herself in the same category as Christ's Forerunner indicated a depth of spiritual pride that is offensive to God.

As her pastor, I offered some guidance and constructive criticism regarding her harsh tone and superior demeanor. Unfortunately, Mary was unwilling to hear my counsel. She left the church. Like Andrew, I told her that if she was to go to the next level God had for her, she would need to change her tone and temper. If not, she would be forever hindered and unable to serve the Body of Christ as God intended. And so, she was.

Sadly, this so-called prophet has lost all credibility with the people who know her the best. Instead, she became known as a toxic person who most people prefer to avoid.

Unfortunately, Andrew and Mary, and so many others, refused the touch of the Great Physician on their way to the next level. He had them on his operating table. He knew there were things in them that had to be broken and healed. It was a painful process. It hurts to have someone tell you things about yourself that are offensive and embarrassing; it hurts to be confronted with certain realities about your competency—or lack thereof. But if we don't allow the doctor to do his corrective surgery—if we scurry down off the gurney as did Andrew and Mary—we could end up spiritually, emotionally and mentally disabled for the rest of our lives.

Do you have deficiencies that are holding you back? Can you see them? Do you know what needs to be corrected? Or, are you blissfully ignorant? This brings us to the next important question.

Question #2: Do I know what I don't know?

Psychology identifies four stages in the process of increasing competency. These are also known as the four stages of learning: unconscious incompetence, conscious incompetence, conscious competence, and unconscious competence.

At the bottom is unconscious incompetence. This poor guy doesn't even realize his own deficiencies. He doesn't know what he doesn't know. He goes on and on in his inefficient, nonproductive manner, unaware that he is completely failing. It's a blissful ignorance. Sadly, he will be offended that no one appreciates him and will often complain that his hard work is unrecognized. Before this person can ever go to the next level, he must become aware of his own incompetence and recognize the need for new skills.

Next is conscious incompetence. This is the person who is failing, but, fortunately, knows he is failing. He knows what he doesn't know. He doesn't blame others for his failure because he understands the reason is his own incompetence. As a result, he wants help, and is determined to improve himself. The Holy Spirit can work with this man because he is teachable, wants to go higher and is willing to humble himself to get there. This person is moving toward the next level.

Then there is conscious competence. This is what happens when a person has learned a new competency, but demonstrating those skills do not yet come naturally. He has been teachable, he has submitted to instruction and has implemented necessary changes in his performance. But the new skills are still forced behaviors. It's a level of competence that requires focus and concentration. It's not natural. There is an understanding of what must be done to succeed, but it's only through strong conscious effort that the new skill is executed.

Finally, there is unconscious competence. This is the kind of efficiency that seems to come naturally. This person has dedicated himself so diligently to learning, developing and honing a new competency, that it can be done almost unconsciously. He has had so much practice, that the new skill is "second nature."

God is trying to bring each of us to a level of unconscious competence. Where effective living, serving, leading, and loving is second nature. It's a place where our efficiency and impact is effortless. It comes without thinking. But this level of competence does not "just happen." It happens because teachable people have come to recognize their own deficiencies. They "know what they don't know." They don't pretend to have all the answers and reject voices of criticism and concern that God uses as surgical instruments of correction. They submit to God's gracious attempts to repair their disabilities.

Question #3: Have I been resisting God's attempts to correct my deficiencies?

Discerning people understand an important truth. Not everyone who applauds you is being your friend and not everyone who opposes you is being your enemy. In fact, those who are friends to your weakness are enemies to your greatness. By comforting your deficiencies, they actually undermine your potential. Proverbs 27:6 says, "*Faithful are the wounds of a friend, but the kisses of an enemy are deceitful.*"

Pop culture is toxic. We are surrounded by an endless supply of sycophantic pabulum that feeds our narcissistic self-deception. Twitter, Facebook, Snapchat, and Instagram are full of cute memes and colorful graphics that patronize our entitlement with the belief that we "deserve" success. Even worse, we are told that if anything challenges our pampered idealism should be rejected as a hostile adversary.

Perhaps you've seen this messaging: "Surround yourself with people who build you up and inspire you;" "Make a conscious effort to surround yourself with positive, nourishing, and uplifting people who believe in you, encourage you to go after your dreams and applaud your victories;" "Fill your life with people who see your worth and applaud you, stay away from those who pull you down." And then there's the ubiquitous quote from Oprah Winfrey: "Surround yourself with only people who are going to lift you higher. Life is already filled with those who want to bring you down."

While I agree we should avoid venomous people who bolster their own self-worth by diminishing the value of others, we should not mistake "the wounds of a friend" as something intended to "bring you down." What if your dreams are irresponsible? What if your skills are weak and deficient? What if your attitude is bad, your demeanor is narcissistic and your ambitions are egotistical? Do you prefer to have people "applaud" and encourage you to "go after your dreams?" Would you want to be enabled to "go higher" even if those heights damage your integrity and could result in your downfall? Or, would you hope to have people around you that care enough and are strong enough to challenge and correct you?

Any quick study of leaders who failed and executives who crashed have a common characteristic: They surrounded themselves with sycophants who stroked their egos. They want to perpetuate the myth that they are demi-gods and seek out people who are less knowledgeable and less inclined to disagree with them. By contrast, smart people surround themselves with smarter people who are willing to challenge them.

This is why James 4:19 tells us: "*Humble yourselves in the sight of the Lord, and He will lift you up.*" Humility precedes the next level because it's only with humility that one can receive correction and pursue the competency that is required.

Sadly, most of us think we are humble, simply because we submit to God's authority over our lives. But submission to God is not true humility. The true test of humility is how well you can submit to people. Andrew Murray wrote: "It's not our humility before God that matters, anyone can do that; it's our humility before others that proves if our humility before God is real." It's our ability to submit to the correction—and criticism—offered by people that reveals our humility and determines if our deficiencies can be corrected and if we will qualify for the next level.

How do you respond to criticism? Can you take advice? What do you do when told "No, you can't do that?" Is your reaction, "Who do you think you are? Don't you know who I am and how God uses me?" If that is how you respond, you're not demonstrating humility and are resisting God's attempts to qualify you for the next level.

David: A Model for Increasing Competence

Competence is about ability and fitness for the task and it's an essential factor in going to the next level. Consider David. When Samuel the prophet came to his home in 1 Samuel 16 to anoint him as the next king of Israel, David was not yet fit for the role. He was just a shepherd boy from the country, the youngest of his seven siblings. But regardless of his shortcomings, God still chose him and set him on a pathway that was preparing him for the level to which God would bring him.

Competence Requires Preparation

"*Thus Jesse made seven of his sons pass before Samuel. And Samuel said to Jesse, 'The LORD has not chosen these.' And Samuel said to Jesse, 'Are all the young men here?' Then he said, 'There remains yet the youngest, and there he is, keeping the sheep.' And Samuel said to Jesse, 'Send and bring him. For we will not sit down till he comes here.' So he sent and brought him in. Now he was ruddy, with bright eyes, and good-looking. And the LORD said, 'Arise, anoint him; for this is the one!' Then Samuel took the horn of oil and anointed him in the midst of his brothers; and the Spirit of the LORD came upon David from that day forward. So Samuel arose and went to Ramah.*" - 1 Samuel 16:10-13

Unlike many who feel some anointing or calling from God, David did not rush to promote himself. He did not march into Saul's throne room and demand the older king to step aside. David did the exact opposite. He went right back to that hillside with his few sheep and remained faithful to the work God had already put in his hands. And in that faithfulness came David's competence for the next level.

Lions would come. Bears would come. In those battles, David would learn courage and skill with a sling. There would be long, lonely, frightening nights, but David would face his fears and learn to trust the Lord as His Shepherd. Working in obscurity would teach him humility. Caring for sheep would teach him patience and compassion. Watching his brothers go to war while he stayed at home would force him to overcome pride, entitlement, and feelings of resentment. Through it all, he learned faith. He discovered that the Lord is his Rock, his Strong Tower, and that God will work through the one who trusts in Him and serves Him with integrity.

When the opportunity named Goliath presented itself, no one on that battlefield was prepared like David. Because of his history with the lion and the bear, and his skill with a sling protecting those sheep, David knew the giant could be defeated. Because of his intimacy with God obtained in those lonely wilderness nights, David had faith that God would protect him. David's preparation gave him a confidence and authority that distinguished him as a proven leader. It was Goliath that propelled David to the next level, but only because he was prepared.

Tanzanian marathon runner Juma Ikangaa said, "The will to win means nothing without the will to prepare." No one ever gets to the next level without preparation. The issue is competency: the ability a person has that enables him or her to do a job successfully. Core competencies are those basic, essential skills an individual must have that are vital to success. Without them, any ascent to the next level will be short-lived and failure is almost guaranteed.

Abraham Lincoln said, "If I had ten hours to chop down a tree, I'd spend the first nine sharpening my ax." Competence is not merely swinging an ax hard and fast, it's preparing the ax so that each swing makes the greatest impact. Unfortunately, many people disqualify themselves from the next level because they fail to sharpen their edge—rather than maximizing their impact by upgrading their competencies, they become complacent in a comfort zone, retract their diligence, and diminish their value. They allow themselves to become "dull." Preparation is not a one-time-thing, limited to one's graduate or post graduate studies. Preparation is perpetual. It must occur at every level. The danger is to become complacent and neglect to stay sharp. The following are several points to guard us from a dull edge.

Don't get stuck in a comfort zone. It's possible to become so comfortable in our accomplishments that we forget the importance of upgrading ourselves. Skill sets have a shelf life. Technology is always improving, culture is always changing, fads and trends are constantly in flux. Those who fail to upgrade themselves become obsolete before their own eyes.

Don't be a typewriter person in a laptop world. I once had a secretary who refused to learn computer skills and database protocols. She was great on a typewriter and taking shorthand, but had no idea how to set up or use the new database established for our office. She was content to remain a typewriter person in a laptop world. Unfortunately, her refusal to upgrade her skills forced others to do work that she should have been able to do. That meant her value diminished and she became more of a liability. In a very short time, I had to "restructure" our office, demote her to lower position, cut her hours, and hire an office manager with the skills we needed.

Don't make yourself obsolete by failing to upgrade. Read books, take classes, volunteer to gain experience, build your resume—do what is required to improve yourself mentally, professionally, physically, and even spiritually. Competent people are prepared. They continually improve their competency through a personal determination to excel beyond the level they are currently at. Too many people are content to maintain status quo. They are happy to simply hold a title and go through "the motions." What they don't understand is that their complacency is diminishing their value. Their edge is getting dull.

Don't depreciate your value. Be an appreciating asset; add value to your value. In terms of profit and loss, you're an asset to the organization you serve. In finance, when assets appreciate, they gain value and are worth more. When they lose value, they depreciate—when that happens we relieve ourselves of them. In other words, we fire them. It's amazing how many people get fired and never saw it coming. They thought every was fine but didn't realize they had failed to upgrade themselves, lost value, became obsolete, and depreciated in value.

Don't withdraw value from yourself. Too often, people withdraw value from themselves. They get disappointed and discouraged in their work and withdraw value from themselves. When they started out, they were excited. They worked hard, volunteered for projects, put in overtime. But in time, their expectations were not met. Perhaps a boss offended them or the company disappointed them, and they lost motivation. As a result, they developed a bad attitude, started complaining and became resentful. They stopped working hard, stopped coming in early, stopped volunteering, and became a depreciated asset. In fact, they become a performance problem and are now fighting to keep their job.

Don't expect to be paid more than you're worth. Diligent people understand they don't get paid by the hour, they get paid for the value they bring to the hour. When you stop bringing value to the hour, you depreciate. I had one employee who kept pressing me for more compensation. However, I knew he was already being compensated commensurate to the value he was bringing to the organization. I helped him to realize that if he wanted to be paid more, he should bring more value to the hours he was working, and demonstrate his increased value. If you're negotiating for a raise, don't whine about your pay; remind the decision maker of all you do, all you've done, all you plan to do, how much value you add to the business, and how you're an essential asset.

Don't become low hanging fruit. "Low hanging fruit" is the fruit lowest on the tree that is the first to get plucked. When the time comes for cutbacks, restructuring, or layoffs, you should not to be the first person that management thinks of. Don't be the one that everyone knows has a bad attitude, complains about conditions, spreads gossip, and has a sloppy, poor work ethic. Managers, very quickly, get an idea of who adds value and who doesn't. You don't want opinions to be formed about you that present you as a dangling fruit. Instead, be diligent. Make yourself indispensable—make sure you're not the first person they talk about when talk about cutting staff.

Competence Requires Anointing

"*And the LORD said, 'Arise, anoint him; for this is the one!' Then Samuel took the horn of oil and anointed him in the midst of his brothers; and the Spirit of the LORD came upon David from that day forward.*"

As followers of Christ, it's important to understand that competence is not merely a human function, it's also a spiritual quality.

The primary element of David's competence flowed from an "anointing." More specifically, Verse 13 tells us that David was "anointed" for his promotion before he was placed in the palace.

This is exactly what we need in order to go to our next level, but the anointing we must have is different than what David received. Our anointing comes by "putting on Christ" as stated in Romans 13:14: "*Put on the Lord Jesus Christ, and make no provision for the flesh, to fulfill its lusts.*"

The term "Christ" means "anointed one." The word Christian comes from a Greek word meaning "little Christ" or little anointed ones. That is not to say that Christians are little divine beings—absolutely not. What it means is, we are "of Christ." We are in Him, and in Him we live and move and have our being. If we are to walk in excellence as David did, to the glory of God, we need to put on Christ, who is our anointing.

Understand, the environment in which David worked was not a favorable one. In the very next verse (1 Samuel 16:14) we discover that his future boss, King Saul was not only without the Spirit of God, but an evil spirit was controlling him. For many people, this is similar to their own work environment. All around them, above them, below them, are people who are hostile, ungodly, and seemingly controlled by demonic spirits. But because David had God's anointing on his life, that hostile environment did not discourage, damage, or defeat him. In fact, the darkness around him only made him shine brighter.

If you go into your environment without putting on Christ, you will become that environment. You will start to conform. Their attitudes, their grumbling, complaining, and bad spirit will influence you. Instead of being the thermostat, controlling the environment, you become the thermometer, reflecting the environment. You will start talking like them, acting like them, being like them. Before long, you will settle for mediocrity and substandard performance, and excellence will be a forgotten concept.

However, if you put on Christ, if you "get anointed" before you get there, you will not only survive, you will thrive. The greater the darkness, the brighter your light will shine. Your excellence will stand out. Before you leave the house, take time to dress yourself spiritually. We spend plenty of time preparing ourselves physically. We eat breakfast, drink coffee, put on makeup, try on two to three outfits before finding the right one, but do we take time to put on the armor of God? If you let God dress you and anoint you with the helmet of salvation, the breastplate of righteousness, the belt of truth, and the shield of faith, you will be ready to stand. Like David, when Saul throws the spears at you and the demons start manifesting against you, there will be a sweet sound of excellence flowing form your spirit to transform the atmosphere.

By contrast, if you get up in the morning complaining and murmuring about your job, your pay, your coworkers, your boss, you're actually undressing yourself spiritually. You're making yourself vulnerable to every attack that comes because you've ripped off your armor. There's nothing wrong with working with devils—David did it. What's wrong is going to work naked—spiritually naked. If you're dressed properly, you can work with anything. You can work with anthrax, with small pox, with nuclear material. You can walk into a burning building if you're dressed with the proper defense. So if your boss is mean, your coworkers are foul, and your environment is a cesspool of immorality, if you're dressed properly, no weapon formed against you will prosper. God will fight your battles and your excellence will shine.

Competence Is Skillfulness

"*And Saul's servants said to him, 'Surely, a distressing spirit from God is troubling you. Let our master now command your servants, who are before you, to seek out a man who is a skillful player on the harp. And it shall be that he will play it with his hand when the distressing spirit from God is upon you, and you shall be well.' So Saul said to his servants, 'Provide me now a man who can play well, and bring him to me. 'Then one of the servants answered and said, 'Look, I have seen a son of Jesse the Bethlehemite, who is skillful in playing, a mighty man of valor, a man of war, prudent in speech, and a handsome person; and the LORD is with him.'*" - 1 Samuel 16:15-18

Not only did David possess sufficient skills that enabled him to do the job, he performed those skills with excellence. Saul's servant remarked that David was "skillful in playing." He was known for how well he could play the harp. So well, he was hired by the king. It indicates his commitment to developing those skills in excellence. David was consistently pushed toward the upper range of his talent and skill beyond accepted levels of mediocrity.

Skillfulness does not just happen. It's the result of hard work, determination, and practice. Every musician knows there is only one way to become skilled on an instrument: practice, practice, practice. It only comes through long hours of study, repetition, and rehearsal that enables one to perform well.

Alexander Graham Bell, inventor of the telephone said, "Before anything else, preparation is the key to success." Mastering a musical instrument takes years of practice. In fact, practice is where excellence is conceived, carried, and birthed. Actor and director Woody Allen wrote, "Eighty percent of success is just showing up." I disagree. Success is more than "showing up"—it's consistent training, behind the scenes, out of the spotlight, that brings success.

The key to David going to the next level was not one masterful performance. It was his willingness to master a million mundane repetitions and endure hours of long, tedious performances. There cannot be promotion without a commitment to training.

No student can expect God's help with exams if she fails to study. No employee can expect God's promotion if he doesn't sharpen his skills. No athlete can believe God for victory if she doesn't work hard in practice. Victory is not determined by the contest, it's determined by what happens in the quiet, monotonous, lonely hours of practice and training. It's the sweat, the soreness, the long hours, the study. It's pushing through the tedium and becoming excellent in the mundane—that's what forges one into a champion when he walks into the spotlight.

Competence Goes Above and Beyond

1 Samuel 15:18 says David was a "*mighty man of valor*." Valor is going above and beyond the call of duty, even at great risk and personal cost.

Though our charge may not require us to "put our lives on the line," it will require us to go above and beyond the call of duty. This was the kind of man David was. By nature, he did more than what was required. He showed up early and stayed late. He worked harder, longer, and with greater passion. He was willing to do the hard stuff—the stuff no one else wanted to do.

Unfortunately, we live in a world where mediocre performance is the norm. Most people avoid the hard, undesirable jobs that require extra effort and sacrifice. Those tasks are left for someone else under the guise of, "It's not my job," or "I don't get paid for that," or "That's somebody else's problem."

These are low value attitudes. They cause employees to become diminishing assets perceived as liabilities that cost much but lack value. Eventually, all smart companies and leaders go through the task of removing low value liabilities, including employees who underperform and look for the "easy way out." By contrast, to be a person of valor is to be a person of value, a person of excellence.

People with competence go "above and beyond"—they become men and women of valor. In Matthew 5:41, Jesus said, "*If anyone forces you to go one mile, go with them two miles*." In that culture, Roman soldiers would often force Jewish citizens to carry their armor or outer garments while walking to their next outpost. Jesus was saying, "Don't be a lazy person looking for the easy way out. Do more than what is expected, go the extra mile." In doing that you will distinguish yourself as a person with competence and value in the culture.

Never be that person who goes on Facebook while on company time. Don't be that guy who makes personal calls when he should be working, or the woman who's texting when she should be tasking. It's amazing how many people expect God to bless their careers and prosper them financially while they minimize their valor in the workplace: showing up late, leaving early, wasting time and socializing. God does not bless laziness, He blesses competence.

Competence Is Commitment

1 Samuel 15:18 calls him a "*man of war*." The mark of a great soldier is his commitment to the mission. It's about duty, faithfulness and responsibility. As a soldier, David knew he was a part of something bigger than himself. The mission came first—not his interests, not his preferences, not what was best for him.

Competent people have a strong sense of responsibility. They take action. The responsible person accepts the burden of "doing what she can," not because she is being paid or because it's in her job description, but simply because it's her moral obligation to so. The person of competence has a continuous awareness that "it's up to me to make a difference and if I don't act, part of the blame must fall to me." Competence takes initiative; it's the motive of self-starters and hard workers. They are not dependent on someone else's motivation; they are motivated by their own sense of ethical obligation.

Martin Luther King, Jr. said, "If a man is called to be a street-sweeper, he should sweep streets even as Michelangelo painted, or Beethoven composed music, or Shakespeare wrote poetry. He should sweep streets so well that all the hosts of heaven and earth will pause to say, here lived a great street-sweeper who did his job well." Such is the person with competence. They cannot walk away from substandard work. They arrive early and stay late and do more work than anyone else. It's that sense of duty. It's his duty to make sure the job is done and if it's not done, he personally accepts the consequences.

Of course, boundaries are important. This is not to say that competence requires you to become everyone's lackey. People of competence learn how to say no and manage their time efficiently so they can excel at what is most important. However, it does mean that when they can, they help, they support, they get involved. The mission comes first, not my interests. And in being a "man of war," a person of mission, the person of competence, becomes extremely valuable, not only to the boss, but to everyone on the team.

Competence and Speech

1 Samuel 15:18 describes David as "*prudent in speech.*" Even though he was a sheepherder, David knew how to communicate. One of the primary ways competence is demonstrated is through proper communication and expression, both in speaking and in writing.

Whether we like to admit it or not, proper communication is vital and gives the first impression of a person's quality. It may not be fair and overly prejudicial; it may even be unkind or unchristian to do so. In fact, the adage says, "You can't judge a book by its cover." True, but how many of us judge people by the way they talk and write, by their use of grammar and slang, or even by the way they answer the telephone? The truth is, our human nature is quick to form opinions about people the first time we hear them speak, which means we also are judged by how well we communicate. As "wrong" as this may be, it's equally true that people's "perceptions" about us do matter. This is why the king's servant noted that David was prudent in speech. The way he talked mattered.

In her landmark book, *Executive Presence*, Sylvia Ann Hewlett reported a survey in which 4,000 college-educated professionals, including

268 senior executives, indicated how they evaluate a person's executive presence (or professional capacity). Twenty-eight percent of the respondents revealed "communication" or how a candidate spoke as a primary indication of one's intellectual horsepower.[1] But what are the components of "prudent speech"? What is it in the way a person speaks that indicates their professional capacity? The following are seven suggestions for prudent speech.

Foremost is correct grammar and sentence structure. Obviously, one speaks differently than he writes, so our spoken communications are not as pristine as we would write, but attention should be given to what is proper and improper speech. Enunciate clearly and use proper diction. Try not to mumble or garble your words, which makes you hard to understand. Speak at a moderated pace with a well-modulated voice. Avoid slang—don't speak like you're writing a text message. Use proper sentences containing actual human words, not intelligible grunts and noises.

For example, don't say "uummm" or "aaahhh" or "uh-huh." Avoid tired expressions like "you know?" or (if you're from New York) "forget -about-it" and "how-ya'doin'?" Don't answer questions with lazy words like "Yeah" or "Nah." Be confident and speak clearly. Talk like a mature, educated, high-value person.

Make eye contact. In the above noted survey, research found that, when it comes to communication, eye contact is enormous. It has a transformative effect. Eye contact connects you to your listener and sends the important signal that you're fully engaged in the conversation. It shows your respect and appreciation for that person and that she has your complete, undistracted attention. Moreover, eye contact communicates honesty, forthrightness, and confidence. Evasive eyes, looking down or away, signals you have something to hide, or that you're embarrassed, either about the subject matter at hand or about yourself as a person. This is verified by Richard Bandler's research indicating that when people are being deceptive, their eyes will glance away from their listener, if even for a second.[2]

Respect titles of authority. When my son was being interviewed by the Air Force for a scholarship, I prepped him beforehand and explained that he was entering a world unlike his high school football team or church youth group. These were professional people, well acquainted with proper word usage and conversational etiquette. I told him to say, "Yes sir" and "No ma'am." I reminded him to always say, "Please," "Thank you" and "May I…" The people who get the jobs, earn the scholarships, and receive the promotions are those who are well-spoken, articulate and use proper vocabulary.

Be succinct. The longer it takes a person to explain their position, the more they portray an unfamiliarity with the subject matter. They are subliminally suggesting that they haven't thought much about the issue and don't know how to clarify it. Whereas, brevity demonstrates one's command of knowledge—that our thoughts are clear and precise on the matter. In fact, the more words we use, the more we tend to cloud and confuse the issue. Get to the point, make it succinctly and stop talking. An old African proverb states: "Blessed is he who is brief, for he shall be invited to speak again."

Be modest. Unless you're interviewing for a job, resist talking too much about yourself. Weak-minded people always betray their insecurity because they make every conversation, every story, about themselves. They make themselves the focus. Resist coloring every conversation with your opinion, your feelings, what you think and how you would do things. Proverbs 10:19 wisely instructs us: "*In the multitude of words sin is not lacking, but he who restrains his lips is wise*."

Resist using foul language. Spencer Kimball said, "Profanity is the effort of a feeble brain to express itself forcibly." Those who lack intellectual power need to overcompensate for their shabby intellect through the shock value of crude expletives. The person with the foul mouth betrays his lack of education and intellectual horsepower. Their vocabulary is limited, as is their force of knowledge, so they must result to rough, brutish means to emphasize their point.

Finally, never get pulled into gossip. Proverbs 18:21 tells us: "*Death and life are in the power of the tongue*." Negativity and gossip about others is a pollutant that kills churches, ruins teams and destroys organizations. Those who spread gossip are social polluters. And if they come to you with gossip, and try to fill you with their social pollution, you should not only resist it, you should be insulted by it. By giving you their garbage, they express the opinion that you're a person of low value and worth. In other words, these social polluters feel comfortable putting their pollution—their garbage—in you. More to the point, that person thinks you're an a garbage can. Don't be a social garbage can. Demonstrate higher value than that and reject gossip, backbiting, and secret slander in the workplace.

If some person is circulating a bad report, stop them mid-sentence and say, "I think you're talking to the wrong person. Please go to the individual with whom you're having this conflict and try to resolve in the proper way." This is what Jesus taught in Matthew 18:15 when He said, "*If your brother sins against you, go and tell him his fault between you and him alone*." The key word is "alone." If a person is offended, the only person they should be speaking to about the offense is the one with whom they have the conflict in an attempt to resolve it, and demonstrate their excellence.

Competence and Appearance

Finally, 1 Samuel 15:18 says David was a *"handsome person."* This is much more than an indication that David had attractive facial features and bone structure. It actually means that his whole appearance was pleasing. His clothing, his hair, his mannerisms, the way he carried himself indicated credibility—especially in a professional setting.

In the afore referenced book, *Executive Presence*, Sylvia Ann Hewlett's survey of senior executives revealed only 5 percent identified appearance as the most important aspect of executive presence. While this seems insignificant, she also reported that it's the "critical first filter."[3] She goes on to state:

> *"If a young female associate turns up at a client meeting wearing a tight blouse and a miniskirt, she may not be invited back—no matter how impressive her qualifications or how well prepared she is. The fact is, blunders on the appearance front can get you into serious trouble...no matter how brilliant you are."*

Harvard Medical School, as well as Massachusetts General Hospital, indicated that it only takes 250 milliseconds for people to assess our credibility and competence based on how we look. This "assessment" is made, not on physical attractiveness, but on "grooming" and "polish."[4] Certainly, one's grooming and polish may not be as important when measured against skill sets or education, but it definitely matters for first impressions and the initial judgments people make about us.

In no way is this to suggest that "clothes make the man." Deciding someone's character based solely on their clothing is shallow and superficial. That said, appearance does matter. How you dress, the style of your hair, the amount of makeup on your face, and your personal grooming all say something about you. It's called "non-verbal communication" and most people cannot get beyond a sloppy, unkempt appearance.

Some will protest this statement saying, "That's not fair! People should not judge me based on my appearance!" Perhaps that's the way it is in your dream-world of lollipops and unicorns, but in the real world, people do. They notice what you wear and how you present yourself. The reality is, if you look like you have your act together, people will assume you actually do. The opposite is also true—if you look messy and are slovenly dressed, people will attribute all kinds of negative traits to you including immaturity, a lack of seriousness and even laziness.

Does this mean one should always wear a suit and tie or formal gown to project an image that impresses everyone? Of course not. It's possible to be "over-dressed" which betrays a lack of authenticity or suggests an overcompensation for a lack of confidence. The culture of one's work environment should determine appropriate attire. But whether the culture is casual, business casual, or formal, a sense of competency should also be portrayed. Design an appearance that is proportionate to the culture but reflects your seriousness, self-respect and competence. Dress just a little better, a little smarter, and use non-verbal communication to express your credibility.

Competence Requires Meekness

"*Take now for your brothers an ephah of this dried grain and these ten loaves, and run to your brothers at the camp. And carry these ten cheeses to the captain of their thousand, and see how your brothers fare, and bring back news of them.*" - 1 Samuel 17:17-18

There will be times when your preparation and competence seem to exceed your current level. The temptation will be to resent your position and feel entitled to greater status. You may even see others promoted who are less competent while you're passed over and assigned duties below your skill sets. These seasons are inevitable and when they come, it's essential to maintain a meek and lowly spirit.

One admirable quality of David was his willingness to "carry the cheese." His brothers went off to battle with King Saul while David stayed home to care for the sheep and do menial chores for his dad. Did David become resentful and complain, "Carry the cheese? Are you kidding me? Don't you know I was anointed to be king? Don't you realize, I should be out on that battlefield, not my brothers—and you want me to humiliate myself by walking through the camp of warriors, carrying cheese?" Not at all. David willingly, and without complaint, picked up the cheese and carried it to the battle.

It's an important lesson: Don't be so high-minded that you're unwilling to carry the cheese. If you do, you may miss a great opportunity. Remember, it was because David carried the cheese: it was by humbling himself to serve and doing what no one else wanted to do that he encountered Goliath and encountered that moment to demonstrate his skills, excel in his abilities, and seize upon opportunity. David went to the next level because he was meek enough to carry the cheese.

Meekness is not weakness. Meekness is strength under control. Jesus described Himself as "*meek and lowly in heart*" (Matthew 11:29, KJV). He was the omnipotent Son of God. He raised the dead, conquered demons, and commanded the storms to be calm. Jesus wasn't weak, but subdued His strength and walked in meekness while covering His omnipotence in human flesh. Scripture tells us that it was His ability to walk in meekness that propelled Him to eternal greatness. Philippians 2:7-9 tells us that Jesus "*... made himself of no reputation, and took upon him the form of a servant, and was made in the likeness of men: And being found in fashion as a man, he humbled himself, and became obedient unto death, even the death of the cross. Wherefore God also hath highly exalted him, and given him a name which is above every name.*"

If anyone had the right to complain, it was Jesus. If anyone could have insisted on promotion or recognition, Jesus could have. He was the Son of God, His competency far exceeded—by eternal calculations—the level of a mere servant who would die for vile sinners. But he never complained, He never demanded more. Jesus simply carried the cheese. He did what His father asked Him to do and, because if it, seized upon the opportunity to "take away the sins of the world."

Opportunity will come. But it will be missed by those who refuse to carry the cheese.

CHAPTER FOUR

MENTAL TOUGHNESS

> “ ***Don't allow your life to be defined by your hardship. Instead, let your life be defined by how you overcame your hardship.***

Do a cursory search on YouTube or Google for “mental toughness” and you'll find any number of tattoo-laden weightlifters or slick-haired motivational speakers offering pithy sayings and shallow catch phrases about positive thinking and pushing past your limitations. Mental toughness for most Americans is about shedding a few pounds, getting a promotion, or bench-pressing more this week than you did last month. Yeah, first-world problems—it's a shallow concept of mental toughness.

For most people in the world, however, mental toughness is a harsh—but necessary—reality. According to UNICEF, nearly half the world's population, more than 3 billion people, live on less than $2.50 a day. More than 1.3 billion live in extreme poverty, less than $1.25 a day. Even worse, 22,000 children die each day due to poverty. I have worked in the slums of Nairobi, the alleyways of New Delhi, among the impoverished villages of West Africa and South America, and even the crime infested streets of the South Bronx. Frankly, our Americanized versions of mental toughness wouldn't survive one week in those conditions.

For these people, mental toughness isn't winning a trophy, or trying to fit into a new dress—it's daily life. It's getting up every day and walking 5 kilometers to get clean water at the only well serving 5 different villages. It's deciding which child should get more food based on how sick or well each one is. It's the 30 million people living in conditions of slavery, agonizing in the abuses of human trafficking, and the innumerable number of women and children suffering through domestic abuse but force themselves to face another day. Sure, YouTube speeches on mental toughness may inspire you to endure a difficult day at work but that's not mental toughness—not really. The kind of mental toughness we need is the kind that empowers you to endure the extreme disappointments and severe, crushing events that life will, inevitably, throw at you.

Mental Toughness Is the Mindset of an Overcomer

Nicholas Vujicic was born in 1982 in Melbourne, Australia, without arms or legs. After repeated bouts with depression, attempts at suicide and emotional distress, Nick finally overcame. He learned that God had a purpose for his life—a destiny to impact the world like no other. His story has become a testimony of triumph, inspiring others to carry on regardless of the struggle they face. Today, this dynamic young evangelist has accomplished more than most people achieve in a lifetime. He's an author, musician, and actor, and his hobbies include fishing, painting and swimming—all accomplished without arms or legs. In 2007, Nick made the long journey from Australia to southern California where he is now the president of the international non-profit ministry, Life Without Limbs, which was established in 2005.[1] That is mental toughness.

Sean Stephenson was born with a rare bone disorder, osteogenesis imperfecta. He stands three feet tall and is constrained to a wheelchair. But what is viewed by most people as a debilitating disability, for Sean, has become a doorway to destiny. He has used his story of tragedy to triumph to inspire millions around the world. This 36-inch-tall, wheelchair laden man has earned a Ph.D. and conducted live lectures in over 15 countries and 47 states over the past 16 years. His latest book, *Get Off Your "But"* has swept the United States and been released in over a half dozen languages.[2] That is mental toughness.

It's the disabled veteran who returns to his family but learns to adapt, acquires new skills, and lives a fulfilling life. It's the single mom with two kids, determined to make ends meet. It's the widow, whose husband didn't leave enough life insurance, is forced back into the job market, but refuses to give up. It's the divorcee who faces the reality of a spouse who now loves and lives with another, but still has her smile—not because she's happy, but because she's strong. It's the man who loses his job, and looks for another. It's the young adult who battles addiction and forces himself to his support group, even if he's the only one there. That is mental toughness.

Mental Toughness Is Endurance

Ernest Hemingway wrote, "The world breaks every one and afterward many are strong at the broken places." It's what happens in suffering that equips us to survive the pressures that come at the next level.

The fact that you're reading this book indicates your hunger to achieve a new level in your life. You want to be used by God in greater ways, to have wider influence and make a greater impact. But what if the path to greater usefulness leads through hotter fires? What if the means of your promotion are giants named Goliath, spear-throwing kings, dens filled with lions, false accusers in the house of Potiphar, and an innumerable number of Midianites ravishing the countryside? Such were the tools God used in the lives of those who've gone before us and they tell us that before we seek to be promoted, we must consider the process involved.

Promotion does not come through the laying on of hands. It isn't found in a prophet's prophecy or an apostle's special anointing oil. Such claims are not only heretical, they undermine the transformative power of grace in our lives. True promotion, the kind designed by God, requires endurance. It does the deep work of sanctification, grinding down our ego, purging our pride, and making us into vessels of honor useful for the Master. It's a process marked by pain but also with purpose. God is working to prepare us for promotion. For if we go to the next level before our character has been prepared, the next level could destroy us.

Consider the prodigal son. He is a classic example of one who received too much blessing before being made ready. In his impatience, he said, "Father let me have my inheritance," and then received it. The next level and all that came with it—the money, the popularity, the success, the prosperity—was his, and it ruined him. It's the reality of life, especially in the kingdom of God: With promotion and enlargement often come greater temptations, harsher attacks and more ferocious enemies. The old adage is true: "With higher levels come higher devils." Before we can go the next level, God needs to deepen our character to support the pressures of that promotion.

By contrast, consider the Apostle Peter. He was next in line to lead the church after Jesus would ascend to heaven. We see this in Acts 2 and 3 after the Holy Spirit is given and Peter stands up to declare with authority the resurrection of Jesus Christ. In fact, in Matthew 16, Jesus identified him as a future leader among his colleagues. But before Peter could go to the "next level," Jesus had to get him ready.

Earlier, in Luke 22, Jesus told Peter, "*Simon, Simon! Indeed, Satan has asked for you, that he may sift you as wheat. But I have prayed for you, that your faith should not fail; and when you have returned to Me, strengthen your brethren.*" It's a curious exchange, but gives us keen insight into the process Jesus had in mind when singling Peter out for leadership in the next level.

Sifting wheat is not a practice we are used to today. It's a process of separating the usable part of wheat, the grain, from the scaly, unusable part, the chaff. It's basically a two-step process. The first part is called "threshing." It involves spreading the wheat onto a flat hard surface, usually a stone, and beating it with a tool called a flail. The second step is "winnowing." This involves throwing the beaten, crushed wheat into the air to allow the breeze to pass through it. The lighter chaff would be blown away while the grain would fall back down to the ground.

It's a fascinating exchange between Jesus and Peter on the verge of Peter going to the next level. Jesus basically implied that Satan had a meeting with God and asked, "Can I beat on Peter so viciously that he will be completely broken and crushed and see if he blows away in the wind?" And the shocking reply that came from the Lord was, "Sure, go ahead." God gave the devil permission to subject Peter to a season of torment, pain, and suffering.

Here's the important part: Jesus told Peter, "*I have prayed for you, that your faith should not fail; and when you have returned to Me, strengthen your brethren.*" Jesus knew that Peter had a significant role to play in the future of the church. Essentially, Jesus was telling him that the season of sifting is going to be transformative in your life. It's going to change you, to reduce you and diminish you, but when you return, you will have greater capacity and greater ability to strengthen your brethren.

Sadly, many have been placed on the threshing floor, but became impatient and fled. They lacked the mental toughness to abide the threshing and ran from the instruments God was using to prepare them. They quit jobs, quit relationships, quit teams, and even quit church.

A study conducted by LifeWay Research Institute revealed an alarming trend among modernized, American Christians: multitudes are abandoning their churches—and their duty to the Body of Christ. Why? Because they experienced some level of disappointment. The study reported that 37 percent of adults quit church due to some distress or offense resulting from the leaders or church members. Closer examination revealed 17 percent who said church members "seemed hypocritical" and "were judgmental," and another 12 percent said "the church was run by a clique."[3] It's an amazing contrast to what most believers in the rest of the world must endure.

I've visited churches in India where 75 people squeeze into a room that 20 Americans would refuse to fit. In Cuba, I've seen pastors convert their small private homes into Sunday morning worship services, filling every room, every space with people hungry for God's Word. In Africa, believers gather under the shade of a tree, enduring blazing temperatures and hungry black flies to glorify God corporately. It's a far cry from westernized Christians who get offended and leave the church because someone failed to greet them or denied them a place in the choir.

Certainly, there will be conflicts and disappointments in any group where people are present, especially church. Leaders will disappoint, friends will offend, people will be hypocrites. But these are often the means that God calls forth as agents of our sanctification. It's by being offended that we learn how to forgive. It's by encountering the unlovable that we learn how to love. It's by resolving disagreement that we learn to walk in unity. It's by submitting to one another that we learn true humility.

If you've been offended, betrayed, misunderstood or rejected, don't run away. If you're serious about going to the next level, this is how it happens. It's by staying on the threshing floor, receiving the blows, earning our stripes, enduring with patience, and remaining mentally tough.

Mental Toughness Is Perseverance

James Stockdale was a Navy Pilot shot down over enemy territory during the Vietnam War. Imprisoned by the Vietcong for nearly eight years, he and his fellow prisoners were tortured on a regular basis and denied medical care and adequate food and water. After his release in 1973, he was awarded 26 personal combat decorations for his extraordinary bravery.

In an interview with Jim Collins, Stockdale was asked about his heroic survival. During the exchange, the conversation turned toward the many POWs who never survived their imprisonment. He was asked, "Who didn't make it out of Vietnam?" Stockdale replied, "Oh, that's easy, the optimists. The ones who said, 'We're going to be out by Christmas.' And Christmas would come, and Christmas would go. Then they'd say, 'We're going to be out by Easter.' And Easter would come, and Easter would go. And then Thanksgiving, and then it would be Christmas again. They died of a broken heart."

Stockdale then added, "This is an important lesson. You must never confuse faith that you will prevail in the end—which you can never afford to lose—with the discipline to confront the most brutal facts of your current reality, whatever they might be."[4]

Mental toughness is not a shallow optimism that enables short-lived endurance by promising everything will be okay. It's not the watered down pabulum that we often hear in modern-day, feel good sermons describing a make-believe-god who solves all your problems and heals all your pain. Be wary of those who tell you to "just believe and God will give you what you need." That's not faith. Faith is not holding onto a hope that you will eventually get what you want. Faith is not what happens when the bills are paid and all the sicknesses are healed. Thank God when that happens, but that's not faith. True faith is mental toughness.

True faith is perseverance. It's a toughness that refuses to quit. True faith is not getting God to give you what you want, it's trusting God and remaining steadfast in your devotion to Him when you don't get what you want. It's persevering in your conviction that God is good and will cause all the pain, all the loss, all the hardship that you're facing to somehow work together for the good and you will prevail in the end as a better, more empowered, more effective human being.

This is why the Apostle Paul wrote "*... we also glory in tribulations, knowing that tribulation produces perseverance, and perseverance, character; and character, hope*" (Romans 5:3-4). Hope is the expectation of good. But hope is more than an intellectual notion. True hope comes from character—character forged through perseverance in tribulation. It's the ability to push through the pain and maintain an attitude that what you're facing is making you stronger, taking you deeper, and that you're going to come back from this event, not weaker, but stronger, better, wiser, more capable, and positioned for the next level—even though you may not get the thing you want.

Just like Stockdale and his fellow POWs, we will all find ourselves in seasons of despair, even agony. Life will throw disappointments at us. Crushing events will come for which there are no explanations or justification. It may be injury, disease, loss or death, but what separates those who become paralyzed from those who go to the next level is how they face the adversity. The key is not having some shallow hope that everything will be okay. The key is a biblical hope that says it may not be okay, but I know God is in control and has a greater purpose that will take me—or those around me—higher.

This is exactly what we see in Paul's example of perseverance. He had been imprisoned numerous times, scourged numerous times, three times beaten with rods, stoned, left for dead, and three times shipwrecked. He goes on to state: "*... in journeys often, in perils of waters, in perils of robbers, in perils of my own countrymen, in perils of the Gentiles, in perils in the city, in perils in the wilderness, in perils in the sea,* *in perils among false brethren, in weariness and toil, in sleeplessness often, in hunger and thirst, in fastings often, in cold and nakedness*" (2 Corinthians 11:26-27). And if that is not enough, God gave him a "thorn in the flesh...a messenger of Satan" to torment him and keep him humble (2 Corinthians 12:7).

Without question, these conditions would have ruined the best of us, but Paul in a profound demonstration of mental toughness and hopeful perseverance declared, "*... we do not lose heart. Even though our outward man is perishing, yet the inward man is being renewed day by day. For our light affliction, which is but for a moment, is working for us a far more exceeding and eternal weight of glory, while we do not look at the things which are seen, but at the things which are not seen. For the things which are seen are temporary, but the things which are not seen are eternal*" (2 Corinthians 4:16-18).

Paul's hope came from the conviction that there was purpose in his pain. He knew that his tribulation was producing something deep within his character. He knew more perils would come, he knew the messenger of Satan would greet him again in the morning—his hope was not that the hardship would cease. His hope was that every time he suffered, it would make him stronger, better, deeper and more useful to God. And that hope gave him the ability to persevere—to be tough, mentally.

Mental Toughness Is Resilience

Don't allow your life to be defined by your hardship. Instead, let your life be defined by how you overcame your hardship.

The Psalmist said, "*For You, O God, have tested us; You have refined us as silver is refined. You brought us into the net; You laid affliction on our backs. You have caused men to ride over our heads; We went through fire and through water; But You brought us out to rich fulfillment*" (Psalm 66:10-12). Scripture makes it clear: The affliction added quality to the psalmist's life. It brought a measure of increase, a rich fulfillment. It actually propelled him to a higher level.

In its most basic definition, resilience is the ability to bounce back. When applying this term to the human condition, people think that resilience means you can "bounce back" from hardship without affect. They mistakenly think resilience is the ability to face loss, suffering, or pain without it altering your attitude, identity, or character.

But the reality is that loss, suffering, and pain will change you. If you have ever lost a child, it changes you. If you've gone through a divorce, it changes you. If you've been fired from a job, experienced bankruptcy, or suffered a physically debilitating injury, it changes you. Indeed, loss, suffering, and pain will change you, but when character is resilient, it will change you for the better. The psalmist said his affliction brought him out to "rich fulfillment."

Mental toughness is resilience, but it means more than to simply "bounce back." It means a person not only has the capacity to overcome a deeply stressful situation, but is also coming out of that circumstance with a deeper level of functioning and experience. What happens to us becomes a part of us. It doesn't leave us, nor should it. It should teach us, inform us, deepen us. Resilient people may "bounce back," but they bounce differently. They adapt, they change. They are wiser, stronger, more discerning. They find new meaning in life and healthy ways to integrate their hardship into their life.

Paul never resented or complained about his trials. He met each affliction with a measure of faith that God was in control and was "working all things together for the good." The stress, he said, caused his "outward man" to perish and his "inward man to be renewed." He credited the affliction for equipping him with a greater capacity to complete his work for greater weight of eternal glory. For Paul, affliction had value. It provided him with a depth of preparation that would propel him into greater effectiveness.

The same applies to us: A resilient attitude will propel you forward. I remember as a young boy, my father taught me how to make a slingshot. You need a "Y-shaped" tree branch that is strong enough to withstand pressure and attach two pieces of rubber (usually cut from an old bicycle tire) to the two intersecting prongs. A pouch would be fastened to the opposite ends of the rubber strands used to hold a small stone or marble. As a boy, I loved pulling the pouch with its stone in place until the tension of the rubber band could go no further. With the target in sight, I released the sling and shot the object forward with such momentum that it would pierce leaves and branches and anything in its way. The key to this operation is resilience.

It's the resilience in the rubber band that stores the energy to produce the tension that propels the small stone forward. It's resilience, the nature of rubber to return to its original form, that produces the action.

Tension in your life is not meant to destroy you. Like the stone in the slingshot, it's meant to propel you forward. It may feel like you're being pulled back, taking steps further away from what you believe God has called you to do, further back from your goals, further back from your destiny, further back from where you thought you should be. You may be under tension and stress, but don't lose heart. It's all part of the process.

God has you in the slingshot. The very thing that is causing that tension, stress and worry, and is seeming to delay your life, could be the very thing that God uses to shoot you forward.

Serving as a youth pastor early in my ministry in New Jersey, it was revealed that my senior pastor had been having affairs with multiple women in the church. After losing his credentials and leaving the church, I was appointed as the interim pastor. It was the most difficult, painful period of my life. Those whom we considered friends were devastated by the pastor's affairs and vented their anger on me. Many left the church. We were mocked by the community. Our building projected came to a halt and the school board from whom we rented space during our building project refused to renew the lease.

After that interim period closed, I took a position at another church in New York. My wife and I thought this would be a period of renewal and healing. The church seemed stable and the pastor was an older man with many years in ministry. We settled into, what we thought would be, a period of growth and learning. Unfortunately, the growth and learning came in a very unexpected way. Due to immorality, our new pastor was forced to resign the church and, again, I found myself as an interim pastor over a wounded, angry congregation. What made it even worse, the pastor who resigned started a new church, on the same street about 10 minutes down the street.

Talk about being in a slingshot. We thought we were moving forward; instead it felt like we kept being pulled backward. It was a period of several years where we were under constant stress, constant tension. Everyday there would be some kind of disappointment, conflict and even accusations. But what we soon discovered was that being in stress, tension and conflict was exactly where God wanted us to be. In fact, he was going to use that tension to propel us forward.

Out of these seasons in our lives came our deepest, most profound growth. Not only did we learn vital lessons about authenticity, servant leadership, integrity, and humility, we developed core competencies that would stay with us for years to come. Things you cannot learn in a university or by taking a course. It was by enduring that we developed a credibility among our congregation, the community around us, and even our district leaders. Add to that, these were the experiences that gave birth to Global Leadership Training, numerous books, and our emphasis on training leaders in matters of character.

Jeremiah said, the greatest thing that can happen to a man is for him to bear the yoke in his youth (Lamentations 3:27). It's these times of pain and hardship that give us the capacity to stand firm in future seasons of pressure and adversity, when there is more at stake and the costs are greater.

Theodore Roosevelt famously said, "If there is not the war, you don't get the great general; if there is not a great occasion, you don't get a great statesman; if Lincoln had lived in a time of peace, no one would have known his name." It took a Goliath to qualify David and a lion's den to distinguish Daniel. Joseph was made great by the betrayal of his brothers and Jesus because He overcame death. Adversity is the slingshot that propels us toward greatness. There is a necessity for adversity. No one becomes great without being resilient through it.

Do you really want to go to the next level? Then resilience must be your friend. It's the capacity to bounce back having been usefully transformed by the adversity you endured.

Mental Toughness Is Persistence

At the 1968 Olympics held in Mexico City, the last event to be held was the men's distance marathon. Contestants from nations around the world entered the race and stood at the starting line waiting for the signal. Suddenly, at the blast of the starting pistol, seventy-five of the world's best long distance runners burst forth with an explosion of energy and the race was on.

Two hours and twenty minutes later, eighteen runners had dropped out, either through injury or exhaustion, and a man from Ethiopia would take first place. The medal ceremony would occur immediately following to honor the first, second, and third place runners. But after the awards were given and the winners left the field, as the TV crews and reporters were packing up their gear, and most of the spectators had left the stadium, a sudden shout came from outside the stadium: "The race isn't over. A man is still running!"

It was true, fifty-six runners had completed the course. The winners had received their medals and most people had gone, but one man was still running the race.

His name was John Stephen Akhwari, from Tanzania. Shortly after the starting pistol sounded and the runners took off, Akhwari had some problems. Right around the 19-kilometer point, there was jockeying for position between some runners and Akhwari was shoved and knocked down. He fell hard against the road. His thin skin tore as his bones slid against the pavement and he tumbled into the crowd. When he finally gained presence of mind, pain was shooting through his leg. He looked down and could see that his knee was bloodied and swollen—his knee cap was dislocated. To add to the agony, his shoulder was also severely bruised and bloodied and was also throbbing with pain.

But despite the pain in his knee and the throbbing in his shoulder, Akhwari knew the race wasn't over—at least not for him. He summoned all the resolve in his spirit, pushed through the pain and forced his body upward. He leaned forward, put his strong leg out and began his stride, he put his damaged leg out, and collapsed. Again, forcing himself up, he put his strong leg out, and then the wounded leg, he stumbled, but managed to balance himself and run a few more steps—until he collapsed again. This became his rhythm. He would run, stumble, fall, get up again, run, stumble, collapse, get up again. And for the next ninety minutes he would repeat this battle with pain, discouragement, agony, and a deep-seated inner resolve, but he kept running. Finally, while the sun was setting and pain had turned to a numbed throbbing, he could see the stadium ahead.

Most of the crowd was gone. Most of the TV crews and reporters were gone. But it didn't matter to Akhwari that he was in last place. He didn't care about medals and accolades and applause. He was running for a different reason. He was running for honor, for dignity, for his country. As he crossed the finish line, a cheer came from the small crowd still there, but John Stephen Akhwari barely heard them. There was a cheer much more powerful in his own spirit, the cheer of having overcome insurmountable odds—of being more than a conqueror. When interviewed later and asked why he continued running, he said this: "My country did not send me 5,000 miles to start the race; they sent me 5,000 miles to finish the race."

In the report, "What Is This Thing Called Mental Toughness?," researchers Jones, Hanton and Connaughton interviewed coaches, athletes and sports psychologists to develop an understanding on the subject. From their findings they offered the following: "Mental Toughness is having the natural or developed psychological edge that enables you to cope better than your opponents with the many competitive, lifestyle demands that sport places on a performer. Specifically, to be more consistent and better than your opponents in remaining determined, focused, confident, and in control under pressure."[5]

There will always be a reason to quit. Mental toughness finds the reason not to. John Stephen Akhwari found his reason—his purpose. It was to finish the race, even when he knew he could never win. There was something more important than winning, and that is never giving up. There was more at stake than a trophy—his dignity was on trial. A sense of honor that could only come from his people, those whom he came to represent. Once you know your purpose and remain grounded in that, quitting is never an option.

The essence of mental toughness is persistence. It's the power of resolve, the inner fortitude to continue, even when faced with extreme difficulty or overwhelming resistance. It means pressing on rather than making excuses and finding a reason to quit.

A term more familiar to an older generation, one more acquainted with persistence, is "grit." We don't hear that word anymore. The very sound of it suggests a toughness, a hardness that exists in a person's character. It's a type of endurance that Japanese poet Kenji Miyazawa describes as knowing how to "embrace the pain and burn it as fuel for the journey."

Mental Toughness Is Grit

Mentally tough people see adversity differently than most people. It's "paying your dues," or "earning your stripes" and anybody "worth their salt" has done it. They don't whine. They don't complain. They accept the hardship and move through it. Athletic coaches say, "Rub some dirt on it." Army troops say, "Embrace the suck." Translation: "So the situation is bad. Deal with it."

This is grit. It's the ability to persist toward one's goal despite resistance, adversity, negativity, and even failure. It's a stubbornness of mind. A callous, determined refusal to quit. Grit doesn't give up.

Sadly, grit is out of fashion. It seems too insensitive toward those who underachieve or even fail. Ours is a culture where everyone is a winner and gets a trophy just for participating. It doesn't matter if you work hard, try and try again, or give up and throw yourself a pity party. "You're special just because you're you!" is what we hear from an overly -sensitive, I'm-okay-you're-okay, politically-correct, stylishly-mediocre American culture. And that's fine if "okay" is enough for you. But if you want to go to the next level, just "okay" will never do. If you want to go the next level, you're going to need some grit.

Everyone fails—everyone. Failure is not the issue; the issue is what you do with your failure. Whether it's a bankruptcy, divorce, infidelity, unemployment, or loss of an Olympic marathon, how you respond to your failure is what defines you for years to come. In fact, failure is not the opposite of success. The opposite of success is "quit." Study any story of success and you will find failure at the roots. What truly matters is not how one falls, but how one gets back up.

Bill Gates, founder of Microsoft and one of the world's wealthiest entrepreneurs, began his career in failure. His first company called Traf-O-Data, which developed processes for analyzing data, was a massive disaster. But that failure served to educate and empower Gates in creating his first Microsoft product, and forged a new path to success.

Oprah Winfrey was born in extreme poverty to a single mother and suffered the horrors of sexual abuse. Struggling to succeed in television, she was fired from one job being told she was "unfit for TV." Undaunted by such painful criticism, she persevered. Eventually, "The Oprah Winfrey Show" rose to be one of the most successful daytime talk shows in history. The pain and failures of her early life gave her grit and propelled her to her next level. Not only did she rise to the top of an industry dominated by white men, she became the first African-American female billionaire in history.

George Steinbrenner, prior to owning the New York Yankees, owned a small basketball team called the Cleveland Pipers. After two years under his supervision, the entire franchise went bankrupt. Even after taking over the Yankees, Steinbrenner faced numerous management blunders and successive failures. But failure gave him experience in "what not to do." Eventually, he not only led the team to six World Series appearances, but he made them one of the most profitable franchises in Major League Baseball.

Walt Disney was once fired from a newspaper being told he lacked creativity and imagination. Following this he founded Laugh-O-Gram Films which was a dismal failure. Broke and humiliated, but smarter from his experience, Disney went to Hollywood to pursue his vision. Despite criticism and successive rejection, his first full-length animated film, *Snow White and the Seven Dwarfs*, skyrocketed to success and launched an empire.

Steve Jobs is known for the Apple brand and his incredible success. What is less known is his comeback from devastating failures. Even after the success of Apple, Jobs was fired by his board of directors. Undaunted by such rejection, he launched a new brand called NeXT. Ironically it was acquired by Apple which enabled Jobs to leverage himself back into leadership. He then revitalized Apple into one of the most innovating and successful companies of the 21st century.

In no way is this meant to present failure as some kind of a twisted blessing that presents you with new and wonderful opportunities to learn and grow. That's like saying being hit by a truck presents you with a long needed bed rest. The truth is, failure hurts. Failure sucks. I hate failure. Failure doesn't make you stronger—failure can devastate and destroy you.

What makes you stronger is the will to get up again and keep going. The grit to persist, to fight back and try again and remain convinced that you can overcome, that you can rise, that you can succeed. It's the will to redeploy, to find a way, to fight harder, pray longer, and dig deeper. It's mental toughness—unyielding persistence.

Building Mental Toughness

If you're going to go the next level, you must have mental toughness. It's as essential to our ascent as wings are to an eagle. But unfortunately, unlike the eagle's wings, mental toughness does not come naturally. In fact, it's quite contrary to our nature to persevere and overcome. The flesh would rather shrink back into defeat and allow circumstances to dictate the conditions of our existence.

Mental toughness is cultivated. It's developed, much like muscle tone and physical stamina. The following are some attributes of those seeking to toughen themselves mentally.

The Discipline of Thoughts

We are thinking beings. We think all day long. We think to work, to play, to eat, to rest; even at night our mind is thinking as it sorts out information and experiences by dreaming. As we think, neuroplastic dynamics occur. The brain is malleable and adaptable, changing moment by moment of every day. The thoughts we think result in the release of electrochemical processes and the creation of certain proteins and hormones.

Eric R. Kandel, a Nobel Prize winning neuropsychiatrist, has researched the impact made on the brain by certain thought patterns. His conclusions show that as we think, we rewire our brains. The neurons and synapses being turned on and off actually change the structure of the brain formulating certain patterns that lead to those patterns being repeated again and again, creating feedback loops that are difficult to turn off.[6] Essentially, thoughts become habits, habits become behaviors, behaviors become character, and character decides destiny. If you believe your destiny lies at the next level, it starts in the mind.

This is why Romans 12:2 tells us, "*...do not be conformed to this world, but be transformed by the renewing of your mind, that you may prove what is that good and acceptable and perfect will of God.*" Essentially, God's word states that our brains need rewiring. Our natural thought processes are not in alignment with the will of God for our lives and we must work to correct them.

2 Corinthians 10:4-5 further states that we are in a war for the pull-

ing down of strongholds—mental strongholds. Verse 5 says we should be "casting down arguments and every high thing that exalts itself against the knowledge of God, bringing every thought into captivity to the obedience of Christ." In other words, there are lies that we tell ourselves, thought processes that we exalt above the truth of God which ultimately act as strongholds holding us back from God's perfect will in our lives. These "thoughts" or "lies" must be brought into captivity and subjected to obedience to Christ, who is revealed in John 1:1 as the Word of God. The Word of God is the key to a transformed mind.

Resist Negative Thinking

Most of us are naturally wired for pessimism. Faith and hope don't come naturally to us. When a job is lost, how does our mind react? With painful imaginations: "I'll never find another job. Everyone is out of work. How will I pay my bills? I'll lose my car, my home. We'll be out on the street." There is often a barrage of worry that cascades into panic and ultimately depression. How does a wife act when her husband is late coming home from the office? Does she reason, "He must be late because he is helping someone. Maybe he stopped at the homeless shelter to witness or serve soup, or is giving some needy person a ride home." No, that's not what she thinks. Instead she tells herself: "He has a girlfriend. He's probably at a bar with her or taking her somewhere. Maybe he's out with his buddies at a strip club or maybe he's been in a car wreck and is lying in a ditch somewhere bleeding out." Fear takes over and throws us into a flurry of chaotic thoughts not least of which is the temptation to quit.

What about when you perform at work or church or for some project? A hundred people could praise you for the great job you did, but if one person offers you criticism, that is the remark that has the greatest impact. We forget about the dozens who compliment us and dwell on the one who criticized us. It speaks to the innate insecurity we all have. Ever since the garden of Eden when man discovered he was a sinner, we have had a fundamental feeling about ourselves—that we are flawed, that we are inherently bad, inferior, failures. And like Adam and Eve covered themselves to avoid exposing their sense of shame, we have been covering up as well—with titles, performance, success, and image. But how fragile it all is. All it takes is one person's criticism to activate our pervasive sense of shame and fear of rejection, and eventually turns us into quitters.

What we must do is fight these negative thoughts in our mind. We must toughen our mentality. 2 Timothy 1:7 reminds us: "*God has not given us a spirit of fear, but of power and of love and of a sound mind.*" Fear is the expectation of bad. We must might fear with a sound mind. In the face of job loss, resist the thoughts of fear and despair and make a choice to expect good. Retrain your responsive thoughts, force a new way of thinking, generate new synapses that leads to positive thinking. Tell yourself, "No, I refuse to believe this will result in bankruptcy, poverty, and the loss of my home." Or if facing the prospect of divorce, or sickness, or some tragedy, don't allow lies to say, "This is the end of your life, your family, your future." Fight it! Instead, claim the Word of God and assert its truth for your situation.

Toughen up mentally. Don't be a reactionary thinker that allows pain and hardship to pull you down into disappointment and despair. Take control of your thoughts, your reasoning, and activate faith and hope. Hope is the expectation of good. Faith is the activation of hope that chooses to speak the good, believe the good, and pray for the good to come. When you have hope, you won't quit. When you can believe that good will come, you'll never give up. You'll have the mentality—the toughness—to press on. The Apostle Paul said it like this, "*I do not count myself to have apprehended; but one thing I do, forgetting those things which are behind and reaching forward to those things which are ahead, I press toward the goal for the prize of the upward call of God in Christ Jesus. Therefore, let us, as many as are mature, have this mind*" (Philippians 3:13-15).

The Discipline of Trust

Trust is a firm belief in one's reliability. It's confidence in what someone said is true and dependable. It's like sitting in a chair. Before you surrender your weight to that chair, you trust it; you're confident in its ability to hold you under the pressure you're about to put on it. Mental toughness does not come by believing in fairytale endings and empty self -help promises. Mental toughness comes from a belief in truth—from an assurance in the eternal Word of God and what it says about your situation. I can be tough, resilient, persevering, persistent, and determined because I know in Whom I have believed and am persuaded that He is able to do what He promised to perform.

I am not suggesting that we all break out in singing "I've Got a Feeling, Everything's Gonna' Be Alright" or "Something Good Is Going to Happen Today." Or recite cheap mantras of positive thinking given to us by the psycobabbling, self-help preachers with all their motivational clichés. No, I'm not talking about storybook endings where good people always win. I'm talking about real life where bad things happen to good people and there seems to be no relief.

Dr. R. T. Kendall, senior minister of Westminster Chapel in London, said, "100 percent of believers eventually go through a period when God seems to let them down." It could be job loss, death, infirmity—whatever. It makes no sense, it seems so unfair, and God offers no explanation.

Mental toughness is the ability to trust God even when you don't understand Him. The familiar scripture, so often quoted, reminds us: "*Trust in the LORD with all your heart, and lean not on your own understanding*" (Proverbs 3:5). It's no mere cliché. It's a life-giving truth. You will go through seasons of hardship that you don't understand, but the best time to praise God is when life doesn't make sense. It tells God you're leaning on him, not your own understanding.

There will be sickness, financial hardship, death and loss. But through it all, your ability to trust Him must be independent of your ability to understand what He is doing. In those times of heartache and suffering, you must get to a point where you can say, "God I don't know why You don't heal. I don't know why You won't provide. I don't know why You won't answer my prayer. But I do know this: You are good and You are working all things together for the good according to your will and purpose for my life." It's a mentality that rises above my immediate comfort and what best serves my interests. It makes me an instrument for God's will. Sure, we want to be healed, but if being sick somehow serves God's plan, then I'd rather be sick. Perhaps a nurse will be witnessed to by someone who visits me; perhaps a neighboring patient will hear me praying in the morning and reading my Bible and ask about Christ. Whatever God is doing, I am willing to be used, even if it means I never understand it, or figure it out. Even if it requires my death to bring others deeper in their faith, so be it.

Too often we expect an explanation from God. We want Him to help us understand what He is doing, thinking that will give us peace. That is the opposite of Proverbs 3:5. That is a trust that leans on our understanding. But our trust must be in God, in His nature, in His character, in His promise to work all things together for the good—to take what the devil meant for evil and use it for good. This is mental toughness. This gives the ability to persist and persevere, knowing that we are not victims—we are instruments of His will, being moved to the next level of effectiveness for His glory.

Resist Throwing Yourself a Pity Party

In this journey to the next level, be careful of self-pity. On a recent episode of the Fox News Channel show "Outnumbered," John McCain, Arizona senator and failed candidate for president of the United States, said, "I have experience with failure. The first instinct is to wallow in self -pity."[7]

Self-pity is the feeling that one has been unfairly victimized. It's the belief that "Because I didn't deserve this, I should be recognized for the amount of suffering that has been unduly forced upon me." In his book, *Desiring God*, John Piper states that self-pity is a form of bragging. He says:

> *Boasting is the response of pride to success. Self-pity is the response of pride to suffering. Boasting says, 'I deserve admiration because I have achieved so much.' Self-pity says, 'I deserve admiration because I have suffered so much.' Boasting is the voice of pride in the heart of the strong. Self-pity is the voice of pride in the heart of the weak. Boasting sounds self-sufficient. Self-pity sounds self-sacrificing. The reason self-pity does not look like pride is that it appears to be so needy. But the need arises from a wounded ego. It doesn't come from a sense of unworthiness, but from a sense of unrecognized worthiness. It is the response of unapplauded pride.*[8]

Don't fall into the snare of self-pity. For many, going to the next level will require unexplainable hardship and seemingly unjustifiable suffering. Those who get mired in self-pity, expecting others to comfort them and affirm them, will never rise above. They will be like that man Jesus encountered in John 5 who, for thirty-eight years, sat beside the pool of Bethesda waiting for someone to have pity on him and move him toward the water. Stop looking for others to affirm, apologize, acknowledge or move you forward. Your victory is not dependent on what they can do for you. It's dependent on your own mental toughness. You don't need others to "do for you" to make it. Know that God is good, and causes it to work together for the good—even if it hurts, makes no sense, and seems unjust. Get tough in your faith, your perseverance, and know that God is in control.

The Discipline of Prayer

Mental toughness is not simply sitting by and passively enduring your situation. Mental toughness is the resolve to do what you can, when it's in your power to do it. This includes, not only the obvious activities that confront or enable what needs to be changed, but also the extremely important discipline of prayer.

Jesus told the story of the man who had a visitor coming at midnight (Luke 11:5-10). Because he was low on food, he went to a neighbor and asked him if he could borrow some bread. Initially the neighbor refused, but because of his friend's persistent asking and knocking, he finally got up, answered the door, and gave him the loaves. It was a lesson in prayer. Jesus wanted us to know that breakthrough does not come easily or automatically. Breakthrough comes because of mental toughness in prayer. We must refuse to give up and be active in our faith and hope through prayer.

Old time Pentecostals had a saying. During seasons of prayer and fasting, or when believing God for some breakthrough, they would say, "I'm praying through." It was more than a cliché, it had meaning. More than merely implying that they were praying until receiving an answer, it referred to praying through—or pushing past—all the internal issues of resistance that exist in all of us.

It means "praying through" the flesh—through the laziness and procrastination, through the doubt and unbelief, through the anger and resentment. It means forcing ourselves to linger in the place of prayer even if we don't feel God's presence or hear His voice. It means dealing with the sin that prevents our breakthrough and pushing through attitudes that hinder our ascent. To "pray through" is to confront those areas that have been "off limits" to the Holy Spirit. It's grieving over our carnality. It's repentance, it's brokenness, it's returning to true and authentic humility before God.

What are the comfort zones we need to break free from? What are the strongholds that need to be pulled down? What are the powers that have held us in their grip? Herein lies the real key to the next level. It's when something happens on the inside of us and we are changed. We are "praying ourselves" into a condition in which we can receive and accommodate the next level in our lives—the next level with Him. God is not interested in pampering us physically, He wants to perfect us spiritually and enable a greater measure of His manifest presence in our lives.

The next level involves prevailing before God in prayer. It's Jacob wrestling with the angel, Abraham pleading for the righteous in Sodom, Elijah breaking the drought, and the widow travailing before the unjust judge. What good is "success" if it does not include a deeper knowledge of God. Jeremiah 9:23-24 says, "*Let not the wise man glory in his wis-*

dom, let not the mighty man glory in his might, nor let the rich man glory in his riches; But let him who glories glory in this, that he understands and knows Me, that I am the LORD, exercising loving kindness, judgment, and righteousness in the earth. For in these I delight," says the LORD."

Resist the Urge to Complain

If prayer has an opposite, it must be complaining. Prayer appeals to God (Philippians 4:6). Complaining attracts the devil (1 Corinthians 10:10). Prayer overcomes weakness by exalting His strength. Complaining exalts our weakness and announces to the enemy a victim is in the area. Nothing will dissolve mental toughness and disqualify you for the next level like the habit of complaining.

In the book, *Three Simple Steps: A Map to Success in Business and Life*, Trevor Blake reported neurological research that proves how complaining (both yours and other's) can actually make you dumb. His findings showed that exposure to 30 minutes or more of negative speech disintegrates neurons in the brain's hippocampus. This is significant because the hippocampus is the part of your brain for higher functions including conflict resolution and problem solving. Blake says, "Basically, it turns your brain to mush."

Complaining comes easy to us. Whether it's a difficult boss, unfair working conditions, a relationship issue, or health problems, we often find ourselves uttering complaints without even thinking about it. It's a natural human response that requires little effort and makes us cognitively complacent.

Blake's research revealed that by complaining, we empower the negative rather than the positive and become mentally weaker and dumber. Rather than expanding our neural processes by thinking critically or creatively seeking solutions, complaining diminishes our capacity and robs us of the ability to solve problems and discover answers. It makes us intellectually lazy and confines us to a defeated, downtrodden, negative place.

Oddly, some people prefer complaining over finding solutions. It makes them feel better about themselves. By putting the focus on adverse circumstances or blaming others, they have an excuse for their own lack of mental toughness and feel justified in their negativity.

On the contrary, people of value despise complaints. They see it for what it is: complaining is the lazy reply of the weak-minded. It reveals a person's inability to endure, adapt and overcome; it signals defeat by circumstance.

Leaders, managers, bosses, movers and shakers look for solutions-oriented people. They want individuals who don't surrender but find ways through. Complaining reveals an inability to do this. Therefore, those who are in positions to promote and open doors don't want to see complainers go to the next level. To do so, they know, would make the environment toxic.

Put a filter on your mouth. Don't be sloppy with your words and don't allow yourself to be drawn into everyone else's complaints. Most people love to complain. Rise above the culture and refuse to drink their poison. It requires one to be intentional and deliberate. Control your words, filter your responses, and speak only the things which are proper (Titus 2:1).

Remember, God is in control. Complaining is an insult to God, because it expresses a belief that, either He has lost control of the situation, or, He is doing a bad job. It's why He was so offended by Israel's frequent complaints. It actually turned God against them. Instead of complaining, declare, "Well, God is in control. He can make a way."

Focus on solutions you can bring. If you stay focused on what is wrong, you limit the growth of your own potential. Brain cells actually diminish. Instead of complaining, consider what you can do to improve the situation. Not only does this increase your value and qualify you for the next level, it expands your abilities for critical and creative thinking—skills that are critical for people of excellence.

Final Thoughts

There is value in the struggle.

One can only imagine the resistance Noah faced in his day. God told him to build an ark to prepare for the coming rain. "Rain? What's that?" It had never rained before. "Build an ark? What's an ark and who builds one in their back yard?"

Imagine the ridicule, the mockery from his neighbors as they would daily hurl their contempt at him. He was the brunt of jokes. His family, his children were the laughing stock of the town. But he never stopped building. He never stopped warning, preaching of the coming judgment. For an entire century he persisted; he labored at this work, both building the ark and calling people to repentance. But none repented, except those of his own household. It's mental toughness at its best and perhaps there is no greater example than this Old Testament Saint.

Now consider the striking contrast between Noah and another Old Testament figure, the prophet Jonah. Jonah was called by God to preach to the people of Nineveh. After a brief stint of rebellion, Jonah forced himself to walk the city preaching repentance and the coming judgment of God. Amazingly, the entire city accepted his warnings and repented in sackcloth and ashes. Here is the point: Noah preached for a hundred years and only seven people were saved. Jonah preached for one day and over a hundred thousand were saved. But which man made it into the Hebrews Hall of Fame? Noah! Why? Because Noah had true faith. He endured. He persisted. He persevered. Noah was a man of extreme mental toughness.

The lesson is obvious. God holds more esteem for the man or woman who perseveres than for the one who attracts a crowd. Anyone can be steadfast when the crowd is cheering them on. But one's true worth is revealed in hardship, when you're alone, when no one is cheering you on. Elisabeth Kübler-Ross said, "The most beautiful people we have known are those who have known defeat, known suffering, known struggle, known loss, and have found their way out of the depths. These persons have an appreciation, a sensitivity, and an understanding of life that fills them with compassion, gentleness, and a deep loving concern. Beautiful people do not just happen."

The next level is not a place for those who are easily wounded and whimper away in the face of disappointment. You will not find them there. Those who have given up when the battle became fierce—those who retreated their advance when friends abandoned and the crowd stopped cheering—they remain with the forgotten, with those who never left a mark or never made a difference, in the graveyard of anonymity.

That place we call the next level is for the those who endured. It can only be achieved by an upward climb. John Maxwell said, "Everything worthwhile in your life is uphill—everything." Why? Because the climb is what makes us better. It's not winning that improves our character. It's the fight to win, the will to overcome, the determination to get up and keep going. That's why Paul used the phrase "more than conquerors." Conquerors are satisfied only with winning. Those who are more than conquerors understand that the greatest victory is not a winning score, it's the will to endure. The will to finish strong—to stay in the marathon, even when we're wounded, even though others have already won, even though the crowd has gone home and no one is there with cheers and awards.

True winners—more than conquerors—understand that the real contest is against ourselves. The greatest victory is overcoming that part of us that wants to back down, complain about fairness, and look for an excuse to quit. This is the place where we discover wisdom, we learn character, we develop integrity, and forge humility.

To summarize, consider the words of former Navy SEAL, Eric Greitens, “There are a few things that human beings must do to live well: breathe, sleep, drink, eat, and love. To this list I’d add: struggle. We need challenges to master and problems to solve. If we are trapped in a life where everything is provided for us, our minds fail to grow, our relationships atrophy, and our spirits deteriorate.”[9]

There is value in the struggle.

CHAPTER FIVE

PEOPLE SKILLS

> " ***The most attractive thing about you should not be your appearance. It should be your attitude and how you treat people.***

Do you think you're qualified for the next level because you have certain special skills? Should you expect to be promoted to a particular job, selected to lead a team, or entitled to a position because you have extensive experience or highly developed aptitudes? While certain professional skills are certainly crucial to success, there is an even greater demand for "soft skills"—something more commonly known as "people skills."

People skills are certain social competencies that allow one to work well with others. It's what we call a "good personality" or "being a team player" and refers to how well you can interact with the people around you. In today's competitive professional world, people skills have become a high value commodity.

Ask any successful manager what he or she looks for when building a strong team and you will hear the same response: We need a team with strong people skills. In fact, when some leaders are given the choice between a savvy, highly-skilled prospect or a candidate with excellent people skills and less technical ability, they will typically choose the one who can work well with others and bring good chemistry to the team.

Skills can be taught, but having good personality and temperament are harder to learn if one lacks them naturally. This is not to suggest that professional skills are not valuable—they are. But what good are professional skills if your attitude is toxic and breeds divisiveness among the people with whom you work?

This is why a recent survey conducted by CareerBuilder.com revealed that 77 percent of employers were seeking candidates with highly developed soft skills. Another 16 percent of those surveyed considered the abilities employees have to interact well with other others to be more important than technical skills. An additional study done by The Multi-Generational Job Search Study by Millennial Branding indicated that communication skills and the ability to work on a team are the more highly desired qualities in potential job candidates. Clearly, in today's workforce, technical skills are merely the baseline. What propels people to the next level is their people skills.[1]

The Value of People Skills

Undoubtedly, there are those who question the need for soft skills. They often think their own technical prowess, together with mere hard work, will make them valuable. What they fail to understand is that proficiency in tangible skills is only half-competent. Being proficient in dealing with people is what makes one a well-rounded, fully competent individual.

Great people skills make you a commodity. People who get along with others, especially in high performing teams, are extremely valuable. They promote camaraderie amongst team members and keep productivity robust by keeping everyone's morale heightened. Unfortunately, people who lack soft skills can actually be a liability.

Professional sports are littered with athletes who have incredible talent, but are poison when it comes to team morale. A particular wide receiver in America's National Football League is currently ranked among the most talented in that position. Unfortunately, he is also unemployed.

Notorious for his narcissistic attitude and strained relationships with teammates, no team wants this guy. He publically criticizes management, coaches, and players and makes outrageous comments regarding salaries, corporate decisions, game losses, and opponents (and, generally, anyone who bothers him). The fact that he was among the fastest and most agile receivers with some of the best statistical ratings no longer matters. His negative, accusatory, complaining attitude, ruins teams by dividing teammates. He makes practices unproductive, undermines leadership, and turns high performing colleagues into disgruntled employees.

The reason why people skills are such a commodity is because they have the exact opposite effect. Instead of a selfish, narcissistic attitude that repels colleagues, these individuals are sensitive and caring toward the needs of others. They are tuned in to the group dynamic and if disunity is present, they have a natural proclivity toward reconciling and bringing people together. They are intuitive when it comes to motivating others and encouraging productivity. As a result, coworkers want to be around them and look forward to what they can accomplish together. As opposed to the narcissist who leaves resentments in his wake, these social healers promote an environment that is life-giving, healthy, affirming, and productive—and these skills are always in demand.

Great people skills make you versatile. In other words, soft skills cut across hard skill sets and are desirable in any setting. Though a certain technical expertise may be lacking, wise managers will always want those with strong people skills on their team. Of course, there must be a certain amount of competency when it comes to aptitude, but, many times, I have heard leaders say, "I want her on my team simply because she has a great attitude." The impact you can have on culture can make you extremely valuable and a versatile commodity that any smart leader would want. Dave Ramsey recently tweeted: "I'd rather have a passionate, unified team of B & C players than a collection of disgruntled superstars. The team wins every time."

Bill Hybels, Lead Pastor of Willow Creek Community Church, writes: "Never apologize for looking for maximum competence in your new teammates' gifts and talents and capabilities that will take your ministry to the next level of effectiveness. But before you agree to hire them, be sure to run them through the chemistry screen."[2] The "chemistry screen" refers to how well people "fit" into the culture of your team. To Hybels, having character and competence were not enough; if they lacked good "chemistry" and couldn't "gel" with the other team members, they should not be hired. Leaders should always be looking for people who are empathetic, adaptable, and relate well to others. Their sensitivity to morale, unity, and the emotional needs of colleagues enhance the culture of the team and make them invaluable.

Great people skills make you an influence. The point of developing soft skills is not just to get people to like you, it's to become a person with influence and persuasion. Persuasion is the ability to win someone over to a certain course of action. It's the ability to convince people to change their course of behavior and accept your way of thinking and acting. Persuasiveness is a skill that everyone needs to have. Whether you're an entrepreneur with a startup concept or a young pastor planting a church, it's the ability to inspire others to join your vision in a way that is crucial to your success. Every visionary needs enablers and sustainers to succeed. It's the ability to persuade that motivates and retains such competent partners.

It's important to understand that persuasion should never come in the form of manipulation. Manipulation tries to control the behavior of others through abusive, deceptive, or underhanded tactics. It usually involves withholding information or intentionally deceiving someone into doing something they would not normally do if they had all the information they needed to make an informed decision.

Good soft skills should never be about deception or manipulation. In fact, people skills are the exact opposite; they demonstrate love and respect toward others by being open and forthright with information. Colleagues know their own best interests are foremost in your mind and they respond with a paradigm of trust. They feel safe with you and believe that when you suggest or recommend a course of action, your opinion can be relied upon, not to serve yourself, but to serve the team and greater good of everyone involved. As a result, your opinion matters and you become a persuasive influence.

So what are good people skills and how does one improve them? Are people skills something that can be acquired and developed with greater proficiency? Can those who lack soft skills be reformed and transformed into high value commodities in high demand?

Absolutely. Anyone can improve their people skills. But like any area of our lives that we seek to change, it requires hard work and discipline. Like learning to play an instrument, developing a new aptitude, or simply trying to lose weight, there will be old habits that must be broken and new disciplines that must be acquired—it takes determination and self-control. But if you stay focused, continue to be intentional, and even force yourself to feel a little awkward, you can become that high-value performer being propelled to the next level because of excellent people skills.

Nabal and Abigail: A Model for the Need of People Skills

"Now David had said, 'Surely in vain I have protected all that this fellow has in the wilderness, so that nothing was missed of all that belongs to him. And he has repaid me evil for good. May God do so, and more also, to the enemies of David, if I leave one male of all who belong to him by morning light.' Now when Abigail saw David, she dismounted quickly from the donkey, fell on her face before David, and bowed down to the ground. So she fell at his feet and said: "On me, my lord, on me let this iniquity be! And please let your maidservant speak in your ears, and hear

the words of your maidservant.'" - 1 Samuel 25:21-24

David wanted to kill him. Nabal had insulted him and his mighty men by refusing to compensate for their protection. His wrath was explosive and he demanded revenge. Nabal was so obtuse, he did not even realize what was about to befall him. Had it not been for Abigail, his wise and socially astute wife, he and every male in his household would have been violently executed by morning.

Never underestimate the importance of people skills—the capacity to navigate complex social dynamics and environments. For some people it comes naturally, for others like Nabal it does not. He was a scoundrel (Verse 25), a social misfit who was completely insensitive to how his actions and words were effecting those around him and it almost got him killed.

Abigail, on the other hand, was a genius when it came to dealing with people. Although married to an ignorant brute, she demonstrated a remarkable proclivity and grace with people that not only saved every man in her home, it propelled her to the next level as a queen over Israel.

She was a hero. And her story is an example to demonstrate the crucial role that people skills have in success in life. In fact, there are five major components of people skills we can learn from Abigail to serve as an example for us: likability, empathy, communication, reconciliation and persuasion.

People Skill #1: The Quality of Being Likable

"Then David said to Abigail: 'Blessed is the LORD God of Israel, who sent you this day to meet me! And blessed is your advice and blessed are you, because you have kept me this day from coming to bloodshed and from avenging myself with my own hand." - 1 Samuel 25:32-22

Though her merits are numerous, Abigail's ability to persuade started with one simple quality. She was likable. David was furious with Nabal and wanted vengeance. But, fortunately for Nabal, there was something in his wife that gave David pause, something about her that softened his contempt and calmed the rage in his spirit. Abigail was disarming. She had a demeanor that enchanted David to let down his guard and listen—and be persuaded. Abigail was likable.

The first step in developing people skills is being likeable. It's the condition of invoking a favorable and caring perception from people. Obviously, if people don't like you, they will not allow themselves to be influenced or persuaded by you. Instead, they will see you as one not to be trusted.

Abigail fell on her face before David. She bowed down to the ground and then asked to be heard. This is not to suggest we prostrate ourselves in the dirt, or slobber patronizing platitudes upon our prospect in order to win them over. But it does suggest that effective people skills begin with a few simple qualities to make us appealing and disarming to others.

Be interested in others. Many people mistakenly believe that the way to be likable is to impress others. So, they talk about themselves, brag about their accomplishments, and try to sound interesting. Every conversation, every experience, every example, points back to, and puts the focus back on, themselves. Perhaps driven by insecurity or a need for affirmation, they think that if people are impressed, those people will admire and respect them. But nothing could be further than the truth. The reality is most people find narcissists annoying and cannot wait to get away from them. If there is a secret to becoming likable, it's this: learn to be more interested in others than you are in yourself.

When you enter the conversation, ask yourself a question, "What is something interesting about this person?" and demonstrate a genuine curiosity. Notice the pictures on their desk or certificates on their wall. Listen to their conversations and pick up on certain details that seem intriguing and ask questions. People love to talk about themselves, their families, and their hobbies. Get them to talk and be sincerely interested and you will have a friend. It shows that you honestly value them as a person, not just someone who you can use to get the job done.

Remember names. Fundamental to good people skills is the ability to remember people's names. When a person believes you value them, they will like you, and remembering a person's name is the most obvious way of making a person feel valued. Dale Carnegie said, "A person's name is to that person the sweetest and most important sound in any language." Why? Because it suggests to them that they have made an impression on you—that they matter to you. So much so, that their name has been fixed in your mind.

Remembering a person's name does not always come easy. In fact, it's a skill. It's something we must be intentional about, being careful to push the name from our short term memory into our long term memory.

If you want to improve your skill in name recall, "be intentional." Most memory experts believe the reason why we forget names is we simply are not focused on retaining names in the first place. There's too many distractions vying for our attention. However, the more intentional and deliberate we are, the more effective we become in retaining people's names.

One way to do this is to "meet and repeat." When you first learn the person's name, use it throughout the conversation. Be careful, however, not to use it in an overly repetitive, salesman-kind-of-way. Be discreet, but be intentional. When saying good-bye, use the name one last time while looking them in the face, and making a conscious effort to commit it to memory.

Another way is to "associate." Some experts suggest playing a verbal game in your mind in which you make alliterations to other relevant objects or people. For instance, you could think, "Jack from Jacksonville" or "Sally who's in sales" or "Karl the custodian." Be careful with this, however. It's best to keep these titles to yourself, lest you appear to have a mocking or disrespectful tone.

Similarly, you could "make connections" between the person you are talking to and someone else who has the same name. Many name-recall experts use this technique effectively. They have trained themselves to connect their new friend's name to another person already lodged in their long-term memory—perhaps an actor, a politician or a familiar friend.

Finally, another tactic is to "see the name visually." As you learn a name and repeat it back to the person, concentrate on spelling the name in your mind. Visualize the letters and picture them over the person's head. It sounds silly, but our brains retain more information when reinforced visually. Picturing the name in our minds will have the same effect.

Be appreciative. Likeable people are generous with appreciation. To appreciate someone is to emphasize their value. Abigail did this when she addressed David as her "Lord" and presented the supplies for his men. She showed how much she respected and valued him.

Every person wants to be respected. It's the one, deep need that we all have but mostly goes unmet. Everyone craves basic things like food, water, air, sleep, security, and heath. And most of these needs are met on a regular basis. However, the need to be valued, to be significant and feel important, for many people, is hardly ever satisfied.

Abraham Lincoln once said, "Everyone likes a compliment." Psychologist William James said, "The deepest principle in human nature is the craving to be appreciated." If you can learn how to appreciate the value in other people, in a sincere and genuine manner, you will increase your value to them—and become more likable.

Never flatter. While it's important to appreciate people, never stoop to flattery. Flattery is cheap, shallow, and insincere praise. It's actually offensive to those who are discerning. Appreciation is different in that it's genuine. True appreciation is specific and emphasizes a quality that one finds is truly remarkable and unique.

The ability to appreciate others comes from those who have a certain way of viewing the world. They look through a lens that finds the best in people and they are not afraid to speak it. Ralph Waldo Emerson said it like this, "In my walks, every man I meet is my superior in some way, and in that, I learn from him." For Emerson, each person he met had some value, some quality that could and should be appreciated.

Look for qualities in others that are unique and valuable. Mention to them, and others, how they blessed you and how their contribution was significant. But don't over generalize—be specific and give details. Allow that person to sense the genuine regard you have for them through the details you describe. Be sincere. If you want to be valuable, learn to see the value in others first.

Resist the urge to complain and criticize. Benjamin Franklin said, "I will speak ill of no man, and speak all the good I know of everybody." Dale Carnegie wrote, "Any fool can criticize and complain—and most fools do. But it takes character and self-control to be understanding and forgiving."[3] People who complain and criticize are social brutes. They repel rather than attract. Effective people skills require social intelligence and finesse—the capacity to demonstrate tact and diplomacy in complex social situations.

This is exactly how Abigail approached David. Contrary to her husband Nabal, who antagonized David with accusations and insults, Abigail was socially agile and diplomatic. With humility, she helped him to see that exacting vengeance would actually diminish his own integrity and become a black mark on his career. Clearly, Abigail wanted to change David, but she did so only through grace, charm, and wisdom.

Unfortunately, when most people try to influence the behavior of others, they use the blunt instruments of criticism and complaining. They think that confronting someone's flaws and mistakes will give them the power of influence to force a change. It doesn't. All it does is make you an antagonist and shuts down your ability to persuade.

If you're the kind of person who is quick to point out the flaws in others, forget about going to the next level. Your abrasiveness will make you someone to avoid. Certainly, there is a time to address character weaknesses, but only after we have earned the right to be trusted and have been invited into that space as a confidant.

Tactfulness is the ability to address delicate issues in a disarming, non-threatening way. It's what Abigail did. She affirmed David's honor, which provided a safe context for his ego to receive correction without feeling condemned. Psychologists call this "social intelligence." It's the capacity to effectively navigate and negotiate complex social dynamics. It flows from a keen perception of how people's emotions are being effected together with the finesse to pivot off those emotions and alter the dynamics to facilitate a positive outcome. Such people can sense when someone's ego is being wounded or someone's ire is escalating. They are "tuned in" to what others are feeling and can communicate in a way that deescalates negativity and promotes receptivity.

People who can do this are diplomatic and tactful. They are likable people. They can address difficult issues without diminishing a person's value. Without flattery or pandering, they convey the respect every person needs to feel while enabling that person to see the benefits of altering their behavior. Such people are invaluable, and will always find a path to the next level.

Remember to smile. Your smile matters. It makes a statement. It says, "I like you. I'm glad to see you. I want to be around you." It's why we try to get babies to giggle and love to pet dogs. We love to feel as though we are wanted and loved. This is the effect your smile can have on the people around you. If you want to be likeable, learn how to smile.

A supervisor at a big box store said she "would rather hire a sales clerk who hadn't finished grade school, if he or she has a pleasant smile, than to hire a doctor of philosophy with a somber face."[4] Darlene Zschech, worship pastor of Hillsongs Church, in Sydney, Australia, said the two qualities she looks for when recruiting members to the choir are "the ability the sing well and a great smile." She believes that when people come into God's house they need to see life-giving joy and hope on the faces of those who are on the platform. The smile speaks louder than words.

Unfortunately, for most of us, smiling doesn't come easily. In fact, the relaxed, natural expression of the facial muscles is no expression at all—often akin to a frown. But the frown is the mark of a lazy face. Sometimes, we need to remind our face to smile—to show others that we are happy to see them. It's the best way to make a good first impression.

Even more, don't allow your emotions to determine what you wear on your face. We smile, not because we are happy, but because we are strong. Some people say we should not mask our feelings—that if someone asks you "how you are doing" you should be transparent and tell them of your misery and pain. I disagree. While there are those with whom we may be blatantly transparent, discretion teaches us that most people should only see our smile.

People Skill #2: The Ability to Communicate

Legendary football coach Vince Lombardi said, "Some people try to find things in this game that don't exist, but football is two things: blocking and tackling. I don't care about formations or new offenses or tricks on defense. You block and tackle better than the team you're playing, you win."

Lombardi was saying success on the football field, as with any area of life, comes down to performing the basic tasks well. In football, without blocking, the offense cannot score; and, without tackling, the defense cannot protect its end zone. Strategy and formation are important but cannot be effective if the players can't run fast, hit hard, and tackle their opponents.

Communication is the blocking and tackling of life. Without it, nothing else really matters. You can have a great vision, but if you cannot communicate it effectively, no one buys into it and takes ownership. You can have admirable talents and attractive skills, but without social intelligence and the ability to listen, people will quickly lose interest in your comeliness and see you as an egotist.

Effective communication is the ability to express oneself in a way to be clearly and accurately understood. It essentially involves two dynamics—listening to understand and speaking to be understood. If you fail to do either, you have failed to communicate.

People who go to the next level are always good communicators—no exceptions. Nothing can be achieved without communication. Having a healthy marriage, raising children, managing a business, leading a ministry, or simply having friends, all require communication. If a person is unable to "listen to understand" those around him and "speak to be understood" by them, his relationships will be shallow, his attempts at leadership will be frustrating, and his followers will eventually walk away. According to *Harvard Business Review*, the ability to communicate is "the most important fact in making an executive promotable"—more important than ambition, education, and even hard work.[5]

Abigail was an excellent communicator. Through the skill of her words, she was able to deescalate a volatile situation and bring herself—and her family—into the good will of the soon-to-be king. Fortunately, her example is available to us today as well as other important references in the Word of God. Perhaps the greatest resource is the Book of Proverbs. Written by King Solomon, it provides rich truths regarding interpersonal relationships and people skills, some of which are described below.

Great communicators have an acute sensitivity. The first thing Abigail did when she met David was show empathy for his position. She dismounted her donkey, bowed to the ground in respect and said, "*Please, let not my lord regard this scoundrel Nabal. For as his name is, so is he: Nabal is his name, and folly is with him!*" (1 Samuel 25:25). She was sensitive to the fact that David had been offended by her foolish husband, Nabal. By her actions and words, she validated David's offense while anticipating that he needed to be shown respect. In so doing, she found in him a receptive ear.

Proverbs 15:28 says, "*The heart of the righteous studies how to answer, but the mouth of the wicked pours forth evil.*" As well, Proverbs 13:3 tells us that "*He who guards his mouth preserves his life, but he who opens wide his lips shall have destruction.*" Great communicators don't speak rashly. They speak with understanding and sensitivity toward the hearer.

Before any word is even spoken, effective communicators have a type of "sixth sense"—an ability to put themselves "in the other person's shoes" and see the issue from that person's perspective. Rather than merely thrusting their own opinion forward, they have a keen awareness of how the information being shared, or how the circumstances at hand, are impacting their counterpart. Even more, they are able to pivot off that response with a more favorable approach, often adjusting their tone and temperament as needed. They will talk about their own ideas, but they do so in a way that also speaks to the needs, emotions and aspirations of the other person.

This sensitivity enables them to "read between the lines." They have the uncanny ability to understand what is not being said—or heard. These astute communicators know that conversation is more than just words—it's also emotion. And they put forth the effort to sense and read that emotion. They know how to keep their hearts open and their mouths shut long enough to read, hear, and learn about their audience before they set out to speak, convince, and persuade them.

By contrast, the ineffective communicator is like "a bull in china shop." This person has no regard for how the other is being impacted by his words—he doesn't care. The only thing that matters to him is getting his own point across. This low impact communicator is always bringing the conversation back to what he wants, how he is feeling, what he thinks is important, and why he should be heard. Sadly, this same person is usually left feeling frustrated, lonely, rejected, and insecure. Why? Because no one can tolerate him. He is seen as selfish, insensitive, and uncaring—and nobody wants that person on their team, despite their talent, education or good looks.

Great communicators are good listeners. In his book, *The 7 Hab-*

its of Highly Effective People, Stephen Covey explains that most of people are preoccupied with being "understood" rather than seeking to "understand." But great communicators know how to "shut-up and listen."

Communication is not simply talking to convey information. That's only a part of it. In fact, it's a rather small part. The most important part of communication is listening. It's receiving and understanding what the other person is feeling, thinking and saying before you express your own thoughts and opinions. Proverbs 18:13 says, "*He who answers a matter before he hears it, it is folly and shame to him.*" If you want to avoid folly and shame, seek to understand, rather than seeking to be understood.

One of the greatest social blunders made by people today is talking too much. They go on, and on, and on—talking and talking—long after when the listener has stopped listening. Unfortunately, these social tyrants don't even realize that the person to whom they are speaking just wants to get away from them. Even more, they become known as someone to avoid—or they will "chew your ear off." If you're going to be an effective communicator, you must begin with the realization that God gave you two ears and one mouth which means you should do twice as much listening as you do talking. James 1:19 tells us: "*Let every man be swift to hear, slow to speak, slow to wrath.*"

Listening is not simply waiting for your turn to talk. Too often I speak to people and it's clear that when I finally get a chance to say something, they aren't really listening—they are just thinking about what they are going to say next. Listening is focused attention. It's putting your own need to be heard on pause and deliberately "tuning in" to the other person's frequency.

To be an active listener means you're responding with certain cues to indicate you're "tuned-in" and receiving. Verbal responses, such as "Yes, I hear you," or "I see," or "I didn't realize that," and visual indicators like nodding in the affirmative and direct eye contact, all send the message that you're focused and engaged.

Body language is equally important. If your arms and legs are crossed and your face is grimaced, it implies that you're resistant and opposed to what is being said. But if your hands are down and you lean forward, looking the person in the eye, it suggests that you're receiving and respecting what is being said (even though you may not agree).

A recent report in *Harvard Business Review* indicated that 55 percent of the meaning in our words is derived from facial expressions, thirty-eight percent is in how the words are said (or tone) and seven percent is in the actual words spoken.[6] Body language, eye contact, posture, and verbal cues are an essential part of communication—especially to express that we are respectful and engaged listeners. And when you're perceived as a respectful listener, you earn the right to be listened to.

Great communicators ask good questions. Nothing indicates that you "seek to understand" more than asking good questions. It shows you are considerate of the concerns and experiences of your counterpart.

Any person can talk about what's important to himself, but it's the skilled communicator who can draw conversation out of another and provoke from them a desire to listen. Proverbs 20:5 tells us that "*Counsel in the heart of man is like deep water, but a man of understanding will draw it out.*" We do this by showing a genuine interest in what they have to say through asking questions.

If there is a specific issue that the person is concerned about, take the time to ask about the details. Draw out from them the who, what, where, when, and how. Don't be quick to offer advice and solutions or give an opinion. Most people are not interested in your opinion—most people simply want to be heard. They are not being selfish or egotistical, they are satisfying a need. Talking is therapeutic. Talking allows a person to process information and sort through the details. By listening and asking questions, you're serving that person's need to express and process. In doing so, you not only meet a basic need in that person, but also provoke in them a very favorable impression of you.

Great communicators seek to clarify. Proverbs 12:18 tells us: "*Words that are reckless pierce like a knife, but the tongue of the wise promotes healing.*" Additionally, Proverbs 29:20 asks: "*Do you see a man hasty in his words? There is more hope for a fool than for him.*" Communication can often be misunderstood. Too often the listener attaches meaning to certain verbal tones or physical cues and the result is an offense often blown out of proportion.

Everyone has certain filters through which information must be interpreted. Unfortunately, for many people, these filters are not always healthy or clear. Some people carry deep wounds from their past which cause them to distort certain statements. It's like viewing events through a cracked windshield: Everything is distorted through old scars and painful experiences. As statements are processed through these distortions, they can be misunderstood and blown to extremes. This is often why minor conflicts escalate into major arguments that hurl accusations and unfair characterizations. Not least of which are ubiquitous phrases such as: "you always..." or "you never..." or "why can't you ever...?"

The wise communicator understands that these filters—or cracked windshields—are always present. So, before she reacts with emotion and escalates the exchange, she will restate certain remarks to clarify the intent of the speaker. She will say, "Let me be sure I understand what you're saying, I think I hear you say...," then she restates what she thinks the person said, asking for accuracy. Upon hearing what was perceived, the person will often retract certain statements and clarify their position. It's a people skill that deescalates heated exchanges and brings common sense back into the dialogue.

Great communicators don't accuse and condemn. There will always be misunderstandings, offenses, and difficult confrontations that we must navigate in life. People who can do so in a way that restores relationships rather than driving people away will always excel. It's important to be right, but it's better to be right without offending the people around you and isolating yourself.

Abigail could have accused David of being an angry, violent man. She could have condemned him for acting like a criminal and wagged her finger at him shamefully. But Abigail had people skills. She knew that in order to achieve her goal with David, she would have to follow the principle espoused in Colossians 4:6: "*Let your speech always be with grace, seasoned with salt, that you may know how you ought to answer each one.*"

When you perceive that a person is in the wrong, the best way to approach it is not with a condemnation. Instead, remember that you may have misunderstood the person or misinterpreted their position. Therefore, approach the conversation with a humble and meek spirit. Say to them, "Help me understand something," or, "There's something I'm not clear about." And then go on to state what you perceive as the person's position. In situations where you're confronting behavior that you know the person is guilty of, rather than accusing them of trying to hurt you or be negligent, use the approach: "When you do that, it makes me feel like you...," or "Whenever you say that, I have the perception that you...," and then state how you feel.

Remember that whenever you accuse or condemn someone, they will always go on the defensive. This escalates the exchange and causes friction to turn into firestorms. People who can deescalate and speak calmly and with control are perceived as calm and controlled people who seek excellence and professionalism. Be that kind of a person and you'll go to the next level.

Great communicators get to the point. An old African proverb says, "Blessed is he who is brief, for he will be invited to speak again." When it comes to communication, less really is more. Fewer words have a greater impact.

Ecclesiastes 5:2 says, "*Do not be rash with your mouth...and let your words be few.*" Proverbs 10:19 also warns us: "*In the multitude of words sin is not lacking, but he who restrains his lips is wise.*" One should not make the mistake of thinking that being a good communicator means being a big talker. There's a huge difference. The key to skillful communication is the conveyance of information with the least amount of words possible.

In fact, some of the greatest, most inspirational speeches were also some of the shortest ever made. Winston Churchill's "Blood, Toil, Tears and Sweat" speech was just over three minutes long. Abraham Lincoln's Gettysburg Address was a mere 271 words and took only two minutes. Rev. Martin Luther King's "I Have a Dream" speech was 17 minutes long and is regarded as the greatest sermon of the American Civil Rights movement.

Learn a lesson from America's ninth president, William Henry Harrison. On March 4, 1841, a cold and wet day, he delivered the longest inaugural address in American history. At 8,445 words, it took him nearly two hours to read. As a result, he caught a cold which developed into pneumonia and it killed him. The lesson is clear: more words, less impact; less words, more impact.

Great communicators must be people of discipline who can control their tongues. They must resist the urge to impress people with their vast wisdom and wealth of experience. They must refrain from dominating the conversation and making themselves the center of focus. Get to the point, make it quick, and then be silent. Let someone else speak. I would rather be known as someone whose less words have great impact, "like apples of gold in settings of silver," than someone who talks too much and has nothing to say. Abigail's speech to David wasn't long, but it made a powerful, persuasive impression.

Understand this truth: Silence makes you smart, but many words make you stupid. Proverbs reinforces this: "*He who has knowledge spares his words, and a man of understanding is of a calm spirit. Even a fool is counted wise when he holds his peace; When he shuts his lips, he is considered perceptive* (Proverbs 17:27-28).

People Skill #3: The Presence of Empathy

Theodore Roosevelt said, "People don't care how much you know until they know how much you care." Empathy is the capacity to care. It's the ability to feel, to genuinely relate to, and understand, what another person is going through, and to get involved in a solution. Empathy is different than sympathy, which only involves feeling a person's pain.

Empathy is doing something about it.

People skills are not mere techniques that empower you to manipulate people so you can get what you want from them. If that is what you're about, then you don't have people skills—you have sales techniques—you're a manipulator, just another swindler who sees people as things to use to achieve your own goals.

True people skills rise out of a genuine desire to know and care about others. The Bible calls it love. And perhaps there is no greater example of true love and empathy than Jesus Christ, the One who laid down His life for His friends. John 3:16 tells us that "*God so loved the world that He gave His only begotten Son that whosoever believes in Him would not perish, but have everlasting life.*" Jesus came to us because He saw a need in us—the need for cleansing from sin. He took an interest and became personally involved in our dilemma. He cared enough to clothe Himself in human flesh, hang on a cross for our sins, and resurrect from the dead as the first fruit all who would follow after.

Empathy is having a genuine interest in others. People can sense if you're sincerely concerned about them or if you're merely patronizing them. If you're easily distracted while they speak, or interrupt them before they are finished, if you dismiss their opinions or try to force your views upon them, it sends the message that you really don't care to hear their perspective, nor do you have an interest in understanding them. True empathy is asking thoughtful questions and "listening to understand" the response. It's being focused and remaining undistracted during conversations. It's caring enough to remember important facts, such as family issues, sicknesses, special events, and serious needs—and doing something about them.

Empathy is showing support to those in need. Everyone around you needs support. Ever since Adam and Eve sinned in the garden and became ashamed, every person who ever lived has carried a sense of shame about themselves and tries to cover-up what they really feel on the inside. Every day, people next to you are struggling with feelings of insecurity and self-doubt. They wonder if they really matter or if their presence truly makes a difference. Inferiority, inadequacy, even self-loathing plagues the human condition.

"But I'm not a psychologist. I'm not a counselor. I don't know how to help these people." Most people don't need therapy, they just need a little encouragement. In fact, the best kind of support we can give are simple words of acknowledgment, hope, and appreciation. If you can be an encourager, you can have great people skills.

Be generous with encouragement—it's like verbal sunshine. It has the power to validate and impart worth and significance. Encouragement reassures someone that the work they are doing is meaningful and makes a difference. Try it today. Tell someone how much you appreciate them, how important they are, what you appreciate about them. Be genuine and sincere and see how strong your people skills truly are.

Empathy is being flexible and open-minded. What does it mean to be flexible? Look at the opposite and ask, "What does it mean to be rigid?" Most of us know people like this. They are hard-minded, opinionated, inflexible, and difficult to disagree with. Empathy, however, enables you to be open-minded and appreciate someone else's perspective. Even if you disagree, you can communicate your disagreement without being disagreeable.

This is how trust and credibility are established in relationships. Being known as someone who keeps an open mind makes you approachable and easy to work with. People need to know that their point of view and feedback are worthy of consideration and respect. When you give respect to others, they will usually give it back to you. When you show disrespect, you become offensive and people will rather avoid you.

Too many people today are unable to work well with others. They lack empathy and don't care how their rigid, inflexible opinion is affecting others. They would rather be right than be in relationship. Defending their opinion is more important than building a relationship and they pride themselves in being right. Unfortunately, they fail to see how shallow and inapproachable their inflexibility has made them. Relationship is much more complex. It requires nuance and intellectual depth to navigate converging dynamics. It requires humility to accept the fact that I could be wrong. It demands empathy to force myself to value the thoughts and feelings of others above my own. It requires skills—people skills.

Obviously, this need for flexibility does not apply to matters of biblical doctrine—in those truths we must be dogmatic. The need for open-mindedness has more to do with personal opinions and the flexible issues of life. If you can bend your own rules and personal beliefs, you are by definition a "good people-person."

Empathy is kindness, patience, and tolerance. I once had a six-year-old tell me, "But I don't want to be kind." I tried to explain to him that it was wrong to be unfriendly to a certain ill-tempered schoolmate in his classroom. His logic was simple: If I don't like him, I won't be nice to him.

While we may expect that attitude from a six-year-old, it should never be tolerated in an adult. Kindness, patience, and tolerance toward others is a discipline. It requires intentionality and maturity.

There will always be people with whom we disagree, and don't "like" to be around. The world is full of different religions, varying lifestyles, contrary opinions, and people who even flaunt the very behaviors that we find offensive. The difference between those with people skills and those who lack them is the ability to be kind, patient, and tolerant to those with whom we disagree. This is empathy—it's the ability to value the plight of others and respect their journey, even though we may disagree with it. Empathy treats everyone equally and shows tolerance toward them.

This is actually at the heart of what we call professionalism. It's the ability to rise above personal tastes and preferences and work productively with others on a common task. It's the ability to set your own likes and dislikes aside and be kind even though you're uncomfortable. This ability to be professional is significant. The ability to be patient with others and keep a level head in stressful situations will distinguish you as a very strong asset. When the time comes for cutbacks and promotions, the managers will certainly remember the intolerant troublemakers and the patient professionals who had excellent people skills. Empathy will take you to the next level.

People Skill #4: The Capacity to Reconcile

The world is full of Nabals. Even if you're a David—a man after God's own heart, anointed as royalty—you will encounter certain antisocial personalities who stir up contention, tear others down, and bring out the worst in people. If you lack the capacity that Abigail had to work through these issues and bring reconciliation, you will remain among the contaminated, made bitter by offense and disqualified for the next level. On the contrary, Abigail's ability to navigate offense and mediate reconciliation was a crowning achievement that set her on the path to promotion.

In my experience as a pastor, the most difficult aspects of life are often conflicts in relationships. On some level, everyone is carrying deep scars from how they were mistreated or deeply offended. Countless people have left churches, quit jobs, and separated from family because they were mad at leaders, upset with friends, or felt betrayed by those they trusted. They only way to survive this turbulent complexity of interpersonal connections is through people skills. Without them, any promotion to the next level will be short-lived, for that next level will certainly bring its own matrix of complex relationships, even more nuanced than those you currently face. With higher levels come not only higher devils, but bigger egos, greater entitlement, and more experience with betrayal.

There are five basic conflicts that wound people in relationships. Serving as a pastor has given me the unfortunate opportunity of witnessing these dynamics all too often. I believe, however, that if God's people are committed to developing biblical people skills, such as loving one another above ourselves, we can overcome each of these following challenges.

Conflict #1: When you're personally offended.

In his book, *The Bait of Satan*, John Bevere wrote, "Offenses are tools of the devil to bring people into captivity...As I travel across the U.S. ministering, I have been able to observe one of the enemy's deadliest and deceptive traps. It imprisons countless Christians, severs relationships and widens the existing breaches between us. It's the trap of offense."[7]

Jesus told His disciples, "*It is impossible that no offenses should come*" (Luke 17:1). The Greek word for "offenses" comes from the word "skandalon." It originally referred to the part of a trap to which bait was attached. Bevere explains it like this: "The rare noun 'skandalon' describes a 'trap'—specifically the 'stick' of a trap to which bait was attached. In classical Greek, the noun often carries a metaphoric meaning relating to the idea of being caught in a 'trap' or 'offense.'" If you ever try to catch a mouse, you must have good bait. It doesn't matter how fancy or elaborate the mechanism is, if it doesn't have good bait, you will never snare your prey. The "skandalon" or offense is the bait that Satan uses to snare us in a trap.[8]

Many are "on the hook" right now. The devil set a trap by using the bait of harsh words or hurtful actions of people—and they took the bait. They have been snared by offense and are trapped in anger, resentment, unforgiveness, and isolation. Fortunately, however, we don't have to be snared. The Word of God offers practical guides to deliver us from these traps the enemy sets.

First, control your emotions. Whether you hear about a criticism spoken behind your back or are confronted by it directly, beware of "knee-jerk" responses or hasty reactions. Our tendency is rush in and defend ourselves, but scriptures caution us differently. "*Do not say, 'I will do to him just as he has done to me; I will render to the man according to his work'*" (Proverbs 24:29). Rather than venting our anger toward those who've hurt us, or even trying to exact revenge, we should keep our emotions in check and deal with things on a rational, logical level. Proverbs 29:11 says, "*A fool vents all his feelings, but a wise man holds them back.*" Proverbs 19:11 says, "*The discretion of a man makes him slow to anger, and his glory is to overlook a transgression.*" Proverbs 14:29 says, "*He who is slow to wrath has great understanding, but he who is impulsive exalts folly.*"

Second, maintain a spirit of love and forgiveness. The spirit in which we respond to offense is crucial to a healthy resolution of differences. Ephesians 4:31 says, "*Let all bitterness, wrath, anger, clamor, and evil speaking be put away from you, with all malice. And be kind to one another, tenderhearted, forgiving one another, just as God in Christ forgave you.*"

No matter how right your position, if your attitude is wrong, you're wrong. If we approach the offender with an overbearing, confrontational spirit, we are demonstrating a rebellious spirit which flows from Satan himself. This will only aggravate an already volatile situation. Proverbs 15:1 warns us, "*A soft answer turns away wrath, but a harsh word stirs up anger.*" Conversely, if we approach the situation with the spirit of Philippians 2:3, which says, "*Let nothing be done through selfish ambition or conceit, but in lowliness of mind let each esteem others better than himself,*" then we will reflect the spirit of Christ which injects grace and mercy into the difference and "turns away wrath."

Equally important to the preservation of unity is a spirit of forgiveness. In most circumstances where unity has been shattered, it can usually be traced back to one person who is unwilling to forgive. He wants to hold a "grudge" much like the unforgiving servant in the parable of Matthew 18. In this story, the Greek word for "forgive" means "to cast away." But this servant was unwilling to "cast away" the debt owed to him. Instead he held onto the debt and required payment of what was owed.

This is exactly what we do when we refuse to forgive. We treat the offense committed against us like a debt. Rather than cast away the debt, the person is held in contempt until they pay what is owed—often in the form of an apology or humiliation. We must remember that forgiveness is not an option—it's a command. Mark 11:25-26 says, "*And whenever you stand praying, if you have anything against anyone, forgive him, that your Father in heaven may also forgive you your trespasses. But if you do not forgive, neither will your Father in heaven forgive your trespasses.*"

Third, go to no one else but the person who offended you and "talk it out!" Proverbs 6:16-19 says, "*The Lord hates...one who sows discord among brethren.*" Many offended people have become tools in the devil's hand spreading division through the church by injecting others with their poison of unforgiveness. The Bible is clear: God hates this. It contradicts His will for His family by polarizing brothers and sisters with wrath and malice.

Instead, Jesus taught that if one is offended, the only person with whom he is to speak about his offense is the one who offended him. Matthew 18:15 tells us, "*Moreover if your brother sins against you, go and tell him his fault between you and him alone. If he hears you, you have gained your brother.*" If this doesn't resolve the conflict, we can go to the spiritual authorities to seek fair restitution.

Interestingly enough, my experience as pastor often mediating such conflicts revealed that the person who was accused of offending someone had absolutely no idea they had done so. In fact, they were grieved to know that they had done anything to hurt someone and couldn't apologize enough. This demonstrates that most people never intend to hurt others—their motives are pure. More often, the offended party has wrongly perceived their heart and misinterpreted their remarks or actions.

Conflict #2: When you have offended someone.

In Matthew 5:23-24, Jesus said, "*If you bring your gift to the altar, and there remember that your brother has something against you, leave your gift there before the altar, and go your way. First be reconciled to your brother, and then come and offer your gift.*"

The phrase, "has something against you," indicates that an individual has perceived something in you that has hurt or offended them—even though you have no idea what you could have done. Regardless of how innocent or uninformed we believe ourselves to be, when we are aware that someone is upset with us, we have a scriptural responsibility to go to that person with the intent to reconcile.

Too often I have heard people say, "Well I didn't do anything wrong. If he has a problem, it's 'his' problem." This is an affront to the biblical mandate to preserve unity. Many rifts between people have further widened because both people thought the other should be the one to initiate resolution. But the Bible is clear. As soon as you're aware of an "awkwardness" between you and another, you're called to initiate a dialogue and seek resolution.

Conflict #3: When you take up someone else's offense.

Hebrews 12:14-15 tells us to, "*Pursue peace with all people, and holiness, without which no one will see the Lord: looking carefully lest anyone fall short of the grace of God; lest any root of bitterness springing up cause trouble, and by this many become defiled.*"

An offense is to a team or group as an infection is to a body. It rarely stays in one place, but spreads to the closest members. Very often when a person close to us is offended, rather than go to the one who hurt him or her, they will come to us for sympathy. This has the unfortunate effect of "defiling" us with prejudice and "poisoning" our opinions with unfair judgments and misappropriated resentment. In a sense, we "take up their offense." Even though we were not personally hurt or attacked, we become just as angry as the person close to us who was hurt.

Fortunately, God's Word gives us safeguards against such poison. When a friend or family wants to share their offense with us, the following principles will keep us pure and undefiled.

Remember, you don't have all the facts. When an individual tells us what happened to them, always bear in mind that theirs is only "one side of the story." Proverbs 18:17 says, "*The first one to plead his cause seems right, until his neighbor comes and examines him.*" In other words, having heard only one side of the story, you don't have all the facts. There are two sides to every story—until you hear the other person's version, you can't make a fair and equitable judgment. Proverbs 18:13 cautions us, "*He who answers a matter before he hears it, it is folly and shame to him.*" Furthermore, Proverbs 19:2 says, "*Also it is not good for a soul to be without knowledge, and he sins who hastens with his feet.*" The scriptures make it clear that if we take up another's offense, especially before being fully informed, we are acting foolishly and are likely to sin. It's better not to involve yourself—or your emotions—at all.

Never get caught up in gossip. James 4:11 says, "*Do not speak evil of one another, brethren. He who speaks evil of a brother and judges his brother, speaks evil of the law and judges the law. But if you judge the law, you are not a doer of the law but a judge.*" The Greek word used for "speak evil" is "katalalia." It means to backbite or complain about another person.

Some may think because they aren't the one "speaking" about an offender, they aren't gossiping. However, it takes two to gossip—one to speak and one to listen. The listener is just as guilty as the speaker because he is permitting and perpetuating malicious talk while allowing bitterness to defile the body. If we are going to walk in holiness, then we must avoid gossip just as we would avoid any carnal indulgence. Gossip and backbiting is a disease that threatens to kill—let us "avoid it like the plague" that it is.

There is only one biblical way to respond to offended people. An individual that is committed to following Christ must have a "reconciling spirit." If some offended soul is circulating a bad report in an effort to join others to his offense, the one with a reconciling spirit should stop him mid-sentence and say, "I think you're talking to the wrong person.

Please go to the individual with whom you're having this conflict and try to resolve it in a fair and ethical way." This is similar to what Paul commanded in Romans 16:17: "*Now I urge you, brethren, note those who cause divisions and offenses, contrary to the doctrine which you learned, and avoid them.*"

Conflict #4: When encountering a divisive spirit.

It's unfortunate, but true. There are some people who are, by nature, disagreeable and divisive. They seem to "feed" on strife. When there is an argument, debate or difficulty to resolve, they always seem to find their way into the middle of it and add fuel to the fire. Proverbs describes such people as scoffers, ungodly men who dig up evil and perverse souls who sow strife. See Proverbs 22:10, 26:20, and 16:27-28.

These people are everywhere. They thrive on chaos. If the environment is peaceful, they are uncomfortable and need to bring disruption. Perhaps they were raised in homes where there was constant yelling and fighting. Or maybe they carry an anger in their heart that is always seeping out. Whatever the reason, they the short fuse are ready to cause chaos because chaos is what they are comfortable with.

The scriptures are very clear on how to deal with the presence of a divisive spirit—separate from him. 2 Thessalonians 3:6 tells us, "*We command you, brethren, in the name of our Lord Jesus Christ, that you withdraw from every brother who walks disorderly...*" In Proverbs 22:24-25 there is a similar warning: "*Make no friendship with an angry man, and with a furious man do not go, lest you learn his ways and set a snare for your soul.*" This does not mean we treat such an individual with contempt but that we avoid fellowship that will lead to unwholesome talk. Sometimes the only way to avoid unwholesome talk is to avoid the people who propagate it.

Conflict #5: When in disagreement with leaders.

In many organizations, some of the most controversial disagreements have centered around decisions and policies made by leaders. In fact, disagreement is almost inevitable—but conflict doesn't have to be. The question that decides this is: "What do we do with our disagreement?" Do we turn it into a complaining spirit and spread criticism throughout the body? Do we secretly try to divide people against the leaders and build a consensus against them, persuading people to "our side"?

The following are three important principles to bear in mind when you disagree with your leaders. These will help us to avoid becoming the source of division or a toxic influence in the body.

First, God respects structures of authority and favors those who support them. Subversive movements against spiritual authorities are not God's will. In fact, His Word instructs us to submit to them. Romans 13:1-2 says, "*Let every soul be subject to the governing authorities. For there is no authority except from God, and the authorities that exist are appointed by God. Therefore, whoever resists the authority resists the ordinance of God, and those who resist will bring judgment on themselves.*" People who engage in such unethical activity usually believe they are doing God service by opposing "unrighteous leaders," but they are actually acting more like a cancer spreading poison throughout the body.

Consider how David, "the man after God's own heart," acted when there was disagreement with his king. Never was there an authority more wrong than the authority over him. King Saul was not only in rebellion against God, he was a man suffering extreme demonization. But David never lifted his hand against Saul; he never moved against him or openly opposed him. In fact, when he took the opportunity to cut the hem of Saul's robe (1 Samuel 24:4-6), he later regretted it. He knew it was wrong to express subversion against the authority even though he wasn't in agreement with that authority. Again in 1 Samuel 26, David had the occasion to strike against his leader, but he would not. Instead he used it as an opportunity to express his love and loyalty even though Saul hated and despised him (1 Samuel 26:24-25).

If we really believe God is in control, then we should recognize the structures of authority over us as systems, ordained by God, to maintain order and balance in our lives. Obviously, this does not mean that the people who sit in those systems will always be righteous—many times they will not. However, we are called to honor the positions of authority in the system, even if the people holding the positions are not honorable. In other words, we honor the position, not the person who holds it.

Of course, there came a point when David could no longer remain under Saul's supervision and control. To do so would have resulted in his death. But David didn't raise a rebellion against Saul. On the contrary, David left—quietly and without public fanfare. The lesson is obvious: If you cannot submit to that person in that position of authority, he is not the one to go, you are. You should leave and, when you go, don't spread division. Bring people with you, or build a consensus against the leader. Just go and be sure to keep your integrity with you.

Second, leaders make decisions based upon the unique perspective of leadership. Many times, people resent their authorities because the authority disregards their opinions or dismisses their recommendations. If that happens, don't become critical or rebellious.

Remember that an authority sees things that you will not see. They view circumstances from different perspectives than those who are not in leadership. Their perspective is a much larger picture as they are privy to many dynamics that others know nothing about. The insight you have is only one piece of a larger puzzle. The authority, however, receives many pieces of this puzzle and must discern how to put them together.

In 2 Corinthians 10:13-14, a warning is given: "*We, however, will not boast beyond measure, but within the limits of the sphere which God appointed us...For we are not overextending ourselves.*" We must be cautious against forcing ourselves into arenas of authority we've not been called to. This is nothing more than ugly pride masked under the guise of ambition and will make you a toxic influence in the body.

Third, God is trying to prepare you for promotion by testing your submission. One must always bear in mind that during times of disagreement, our qualifications for enlargement are being tested. How we submit to the authority we disagree with determines how much authority we will be entrusted with in the future. 1 Peter 5:5b-6 says, "*God resists the proud, but gives grace to the humble. Therefore, humble yourselves under the mighty hand of God, that He may exalt you in due time.*" To the degree we support our authority, especially when we don't like their vision, is the same degree of authority to which we will ascend.

Another principle to remember is born out in Galatians 6:7: "*Do not be deceived, God is not mocked; for whatever a man sows, that he will also reap.*" The same attitude we take toward our authorities is the same attitude our future followers will take toward us. Our attitudes and behaviors are like seeds being planted in the field of our life. Those same seeds will eventually sprout into either a good or bad harvest that we will eventually reap. If and when you get to the next level, be sure you have planted good seeds that will provide you with enablers who will be supportive and loyal, even when they disagree with you and have their own opinions. If you're subversive, undermining, and gossipy now, the people who will follow and serve you will also be subversive, undermining, and gossipy. "Whatever a man sows, that he will also reap."

People Skill #5: The Power to Persuade

Have you ever needed to persuade someone to do something? Whether it's getting a colleague to join your team or convincing a toddler to pick up his toys, persuasion is something we all use every day. The difference in our effectiveness goes back to people skills. Some people can persuade rather effortlessly without anyone hardly noticing. Others, however, are persuasion weaklings and ultimately must fall back on the power of the position to force someone to do what they want.

An old fable tells the tale of how the wind and the sun decided they had a competition. They wanted to determine, once and for all, who was stronger. For the contest, they agreed that the winner would be the one who could persuade a man to take off his coat. The wind blew and blew, but the man only held on more tightly to his coat. Then the sun brightened its glare and shone gently down upon him. Within minutes, the man—gladly and with great enthusiasm—took off his coat.

The moral of the story is clear: You cannot force someone to do something they don't want to do. In fact, the more you force, the more they hold onto their coat. Instead, the power of persuasion influences them to "want to do" what you want them to do—the way you want them to do it.

This is the essence of persuasion: It's getting others to buy into an idea, and be motivated internally to do it. Remember the sun. Persuasion is exerting such healthy, positive influence that individuals are intrinsically motivated toward a certain course of action.

Abigail was powerfully persuasive. She made a suggestion and then influenced David—who was enraged by a sense of vengeance—to relent from his path. David was being driven by a passion. He and his men were armed and dangerous. But one woman, through the power of persuasion, was able to stop an entire army and keep the peace.

If Abigail can do it, so can you, but it requires good people skills.

Persuasiveness through People Skills

The self-help market is flooded with books on the power of persuasion. From Dale Carnegie's classic, *How to Win Friends and Influence People,* and Robert Cialdini's national bestseller, *Influence: The Psychology of Persuasion,* to Robert Moore's, *Persuasion: The Key to Seduce the Universe and Become a Master of Manipulation*, everyone seems to have a special formula for getting people to do what you want them to do.

But these techniques are not for the man or woman of God. For us, persuasion is about empowering others to fulfill their potential; never should we want to manipulate and control people for our benefit. Instead, we want to enlighten people and propel them forward. This is what servant leadership is all about. We seek to influence, not so we can wield authority and control people, but so we can use our influence to serve and promote others.

Persuasion then, is not about me getting something out of you. Persuasion is about me helping you to realize and fulfill your own potential.

It's about my influence in your life for good—not my good, but yours—and that of the kingdom of God. Those of us who can persuade—with purity and integrity—are candidates for what God sees as our next level.

So, what is the power to persuade? It's good people skills. It's having such an impact on people that they have high regard for you and respect your influence. To be persuasive is to be the sun, not the wind. It is to impact, to inspire, to stimulate, motivate and encourage.

Each of the aforementioned characteristics—the quality of being likable, the ability to communicate, the presence of empathy and the capacity for reconciliation—have the synergistic effect of making us into people with powerful persuasiveness. But as we seek to persuade, may it not be for our benefit, but for the glory of God and edification of people.

CHAPTER SIX

MORAL VIRTUE

" ***The 'Next Level' will destroy you if your character has not been prepared for it.***

There once was a man who built a tower. He gathered the best material including marble for the floors, stained glass for windows, mahogany for doors, granite and oak for kitchens, silver and gold for the fixtures, and he set out to build. It was a beautiful tower, there were none like it in the world. People came from miles around to admire it. They would take pictures of it, use it in their paintings, and even feature it in magazines.

So they said, "Build it higher! You have the materials. You know how to do it. Something this beautiful should reach the heavens." So he built, and it was beautiful. And he continued to build—higher, and higher, and higher. In fact, the tower was so grand and glorious that he moved his family into it. His parents, his children, his closest friends, all joined him there and made it their home.

But there was one thing this gifted builder neglected to consider, there was one calculation he failed to make: Without a strong foundation, a building will fall.

It's not the marble walls, the stained glass, or the ornate design that is the most important part of a building—it's the foundation. It doesn't matter how beautiful its appearance or spectacular its design, if the structure doesn't stand upon a secure base, it will collapse under the pressure of its own height.

But the man didn't care about the foundation, he just wanted to go higher.

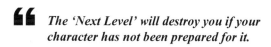

Every foundation has its cracks, and this man's foundation was no different. Usually, cracks are not a problem if one doesn't build too high and put too much weight upon them. But if you keep building, the pressure on those cracks causes them to fracture and split. Unfortunately, what were little cracks in his foundation, expanded and became larger and larger as he built higher and higher. Soon, the laws of architecture began to prevail and his building started to lean.

His wife tried to warn him. His friends shared their concerns. Other warnings came from other skillful builders. But he did not care. The tower was so beautiful, so admired by so many people, that he kept building and building, higher and higher.

As expected, what were once small, little fractures in his foundation became gaping holes. The tower leaned more and more. More warnings came, but he didn't care. "One more level," he thought. And higher he went again. Suddenly, just as everyone warned him, the foundation could no longer support the massive weight of the structure and split apart. The building came crashing down in a plume of dust and debris, and everyone in the building—including his family, his friends and his closest admirers—perished.

Surviving Your Enlargement

Renowned Bible teacher David Ravenhill visited our church and presented a teaching called, "Surviving the Anointing." Directed toward leaders, both established and emerging, he said: "I have good news and bad news for you. The bad news is 90 percent of you won't make it. The good news, however, is this: you don't have to be a part of that statistic."

His statement was based upon a report provided by John Maxwell that revealed only 1 person out of every 10 who enters ministry will still be in it when he or she reaches the age of 65.[1] It bears out an alarming modern-day reality: We are raising a generation of leaders who don't understand the value of foundations.

Many today who enter ministry and leadership know the value of anointing and gifting. They know the value of enlargement and success and going to the next level, but they don't understand the value of having a foundation that can support that next level. Too many fail to grasp the prayer of Robert Frost who said, "Lord, help them to lay foundations strong enough to bear the weight You will later place upon them."

It's not their fault—not really. Today, in both the church and the world, we've created a culture that values gifting and style over substance and integrity. Proverbs 18:16 tells us, "*A man's gift makes room for him,*" and we've followed that pattern. If you have gift, we'll make room for you. If you can preach, we'll give you a pulpit. If you can sing, we'll give you a microphone. Character and integrity don't really matter. Maturity and moral virtue aren't really a concern. As long as you have your gift, your talent, your charisma and style, the next level is yours.

Unfortunately, we forgot to teach them about character.

We forgot to tell them that the next level can destroy them if their character is not prepared for it. We forgot to warn them that your leadership gifting has the potential to take you further than your character can sustain you. We neglected to advise them that if the light that is in you is not brighter than the light that is on you, then the light that is on you will destroy you.

So let this be your warning: Higher levels bring higher devils. With advancement and promotion to the next level also comes greater temptations, fiercer attacks, and more intense warfare. When you go higher, you will encounter struggles and snares that did not exist at your current level. If you're a man, women will present themselves to you. If you're a woman, men will do the same. Money will be put into your hands that doesn't belong to you. People will admire you and inflate your ego with a perverted sense of self-importance. If your character isn't strong enough, all those pressures will find the cracks in your integrity and great will be the fall.

Even more, the words of Jesus warn us: *"Therefore whoever hears these sayings of Mine, and does them, I will liken him to a wise man who built his house on the rock: and the rain descended, the floods came, and the winds blew and beat on that house; and it did not fall, for it was founded on the rock. But everyone who hears these sayings of Mine, and does not do them, will be like a foolish man who built his house on the sand: and the rain descended, the floods came, and the winds blew and beat on that house; and it fell. And great was its fall"* (Matthew 7:24-27).

Martin Lloyd Jones said, "The worst thing that can happen to a man is for him to succeed before he is ready." Columnist Cindy Adams wrote, "Success has made failures of many men." It's sad but true. Too many "successful" leaders have collapsed under the weight of their promotion. Intermittent ethical compromises that once seemed like insignificant cracks in the foundation of a small building, became gaping breaches of immorality in the place of enlargement. Impure motives, like a sleeping giant, were awakened by the egotistic opportunities afforded in success. The noble qualities that first initiated their increase were eroded by secret sins, and sadly, the heights to which they ascended came crashing down.

Their foundation—their character—was unable to support the pressures of their heightened success.

The truth is this: Only when we allow our character to be deepened, will we be able to withstand the storms of pressures of the next level to which we aspire.

From an Anointed Cherub to a Corrupted Devil

Before he became Satan, the prince of darkness, the Bible called him Lucifer, the son of the morning. In Ezekiel 14, he is described as the "Anointed Cherub" and, because of certain descriptions in his appearance that resemble musical instruments, some believe he was the worship leader of heaven.

But what happened to him? How could one who rose to such a high level fall to a place of such disdain and contempt? Though Isaiah says he was "created in perfection," Ezekiel says iniquity was found in him. There was a fracture in his foundation.

Apparently Lucifer the angel was keenly aware of his beauty and great anointing. In fact, the more God used him and the higher he went, the more his ego became inflated and his pride took over. He developed a perverted sense of self-importance and began to feel entitled and uniquely deserving of certain positions and privileges. Finally, he said, "*I will ascend into heaven, I will exalt my throne above the stars of God...(and) be like the Most High*" (Isaiah 14:13-14). His character was unable to support his promotion. Pride fractured his ego, which led to him being corrupted by the admiration and adulation that came at the next level. Promotion ruined him.

We see it all the time. Men and women who find promotion and success are ruined by that promotion. A sense of importance and entitlement takes over. They start to expect—even demand—certain perks and privileges that should come with their enlargement: "Carry my bag. Open my door. Sit me at the best seats. Put me with the important people." They fail to realize that the foundation is fractured and the building is leaning.

Be careful that your ascent to the next level doesn't ruin you like it ruined Lucifer. Before you seek enlargement, seek the character to support that enlargement. Let your prayer be: "Lord don't allow me to be promoted beyond what my character can support. Enlarge my character first—so it can uphold the next level you want me to have. Don't allow me to be promoted—prevent my promotion—if my character has not been prepared to bare the pressures and temptations that come with that promotion."

The Solomon Question

In 1 Kings 3, the story is told of a young man named Solomon. His father, King David, had just relinquished the crown and announced to the world his selection for a successor: Solomon was about to go to the next level.

On the verge of his promotion, God visited Solomon in a dream and asked him a question. Essentially, God said, "Solomon, as you become king over my people, ask what you want from me, and I will give it to you." His response is an extremely important lesson for all who aspire to the next level.

Solomon did not ask for greatness. He did not seek success, prosperity, power, or wealth. Instead, Solomon asked God to change something about himself. He said, "*Give to Your servant an understanding heart to judge Your people, that I may discern between good and evil. For who is able to judge this great people of Yours?*"

Solomon knew there was something lacking in himself. Moreover, he knew that if he were to receive all the wealth and power that came with being king—because of his lack of wisdom—he would ruin it. Even worse, all that wealth and power would ruin him.

If God were to ask you the "Solomon Question," what would your response be? To find the true answer, simply look at what you're already praying for. Many emerging leaders are praying for a greater anointing, a bigger church, more people, more finances, greater resources, etc., etc. Some believe they should be successful business owners, so they are seeking financial enlargement. Others believe they are called to preach to thousands, so they are praying for an international ministry. Still others believe they should have broader influence, wider connections, or a larger network, so they are seeking opportunities to bring it to pass.

But what we need to realize, like Solomon, is that if God does not do something "in us" first, then we will ruin and destroy that thing God gives to us. Even worse, that enlargement and success could destroy and ruin us—as it has ruined so many before us.

Fuller Theological Seminary Professor J. Robert Clinton researched the lives of biblical leaders over the scope of their careers.[2] Of more than three hundred leaders in the Bible, approximately one hundred had sufficient information available to study their careers. This included Old Testament patriarchs, priests, and military leaders as various New Testament leaders. He concluded that only 30 percent of these leaders in the Bible finished well.[3] In other words, 70 percent did not. That means only 1 out of 3 biblical leaders finished well and remained strong and productive for the Lord to the end.

Should we expect that the trends have improved today? Another study conducted by Richard Krejcir, Ph.D., and the Francis A. Schaeffer Institute of Church Leadership Development, looked at trends and careers of over twelve hundred contemporary Christian leaders and found that the same patterns continue today: Most leaders are not finishing well. That study revealed that 60 to 80 percent of those who enter the ministry will not still be in it 10 years later, and only a fraction will stay in it as a lifetime career. Sadly, many are burning out, losing marriages, suffering scandals with money and women, abusing their authority, or simply become complacent and ineffective.[4]

The point is this: Many leaders arrive at the next level unprepared. Sure, they may have powerful gifts, a great education, and impressive credentials, but they often lack a foundation of character to support them through the struggles. And the struggles will come. Higher levels bring higher devils. The good news is you don't have to be numbered among the 70 to 80 percent who don't finish well. You can be a part of the 20 to 30 percent who overcome.

Solomon shows us the key. When offered the opportunity to receive from God anything he desired, he realized what he needed most was to be prepared—internally. His concern was for his character. His priority was for his inward capacity. His foundation of wisdom, integrity, humility and purity had to be enlarged in order to support the external enlargement before him. As a result, God considered him qualified for the next level and, first, enlarged his character, and then his scope of influence beyond anything he could imagine

As we aspire to the next level, our focus should not be on the outward benefits we may receive, but the inward matters of the heart. What is the condition of our integrity? How prevalent is our humility? Do we demonstrate servanthood and selflessness? Do we act out of pure motives, seeking only the glory of God, or do we hope to achieve something for our own ego? These are the issues that must precede our promotion and be firmly fixed in our character.

For those going upward, to the next level, I want to suggest a new way of praying. Instead of seeking success, resources, more people, and more money, we should pray like Solomon. Ask God to enlarge your foundation of character first, to support the weight and pressure being added by the next level awaiting you. In fact, I challenge you to ask Him to stop your enlargement, to prevent you from being promoted if your character is not deep enough to support that promotion.

"Heavenly Father, I thank you for the call You have placed on my life and the enlargement I have experienced so far. However,

I acknowledge that there are fractures in my character that threaten to destroy my life and all You have built. I ask you now, in the Name of Jesus, to repair these fractures before taking me to the next level.

"Until these fault lines in my character have been restored, do not allow me to be promoted to the next level. Stop my promotion if my character has not been prepared to bare the pressures that come with that promotion. Enlarge my character first, and prepare me to be that house founded on the Rock, ready support the enlargement you have willed my life."

The Gold, the Girls, and the Glory

There are three very specific dangers associated with enlargement. They have been called the "Unholy Triad," the "Triple Threat," and the "Three-headed Dragon" that devours Christian leaders. They have become known in various circles under different phrases such as: "PMS: Pride, Money and Sex" or "Sex, Status and Salary" or "The Gold, the Girls and the Glory." (My apologies to the "girls." The intended threat implied is not women, but any sexual activity outside of marriage.)

Most leaders are vulnerable to at least one or maybe even all three. In any event, it's the development of strong character and moral virtue that will empower one to stand firm against these snares.

The Gold: Enlarging with Integrity

Character is moral virtue—integrity. It's a firm sense of right and wrong—a value system arising from a conviction of ethical absolutes. It's the commitment to do what is right and ethical regardless of cost, discomfort, or risk.

Giftedness may take you to the next level, but only character will keep you there. In fact, most people get into trouble when their character does not keep pace with the momentum created by their giftedness. But when character is a priority over enlargement, when integrity is more important than success, one's life and all he has built will be secure.

Proverbs 10:9 tells us, "*He who walks with integrity walks securely, but he who perverts his ways will become known.*" One's life may be filled with great accomplishments, but it's integrity that keeps those accomplishments secure. One may have a successful career and draw the admiration of great men—but it's integrity that will keep that success secure. One may have been blessed with a wonderful wife and a healthy marriage—but it's integrity that will keep that marriage secure. One may be a gifted individual with bright prospects for the next level, but it's integrity that provides a firm foundation to support enlargement.

What Is Integrity?

Integrity is a commitment to principle. It's being consistent in your convictions regardless of circumstance. Titus 2:7-8 instructs us, "... *in all things...(show) integrity.*" Integrity comes from the Latin word "integer" which means "one" or "wholeness." To have integrity means there is no double-mindedness or duplicity it one's character. It's the condition of being whole—undivided in values and conduct. The man of integrity has integrated his whole life around a set of principles. There is no difference in the way he acts from one situation to the next.

A principle is a moral rule that guides you regarding right and wrong, and dictates your actions. Of course, no one is perfect and everyone falls short of their principles from time to time. But at the core, the person of integrity struggles to remain consistent with the values in which they believe. Unfortunately, when faced with the prospect of personal or financial gain, many people willingly compromise—even abandon their principles.

In James Patterson's book, *The Day America Told the Truth,* a question was asked: "What are you willing to do for 10 million dollars?" The results were quite revealing. Twenty-five percent would abandon their family, 23 percent would become prostitutes for a week, 16 percent would give up their American citizenships, 16 percent would leave their spouses, 10 percent would withhold testimony to let a murderer go free, 7 percent would kill a stranger, and 3 percent would put their children up for adoption.

One might say, "But prostitution is wrong, divorce is wrong, murder is wrong." Apparently, these are wrong only if integrity is a priority in your life. A large percentage of the population is not interested in doing what is right in principle—they are more interested in doing what is "right for the moment" and brings the most benefit.

In other words, for some people, right and wrong are not decided by an absolute set of values. Right and wrong are decided by what best serves their interests or ambitions for the moment. "If being honest helps me advance my career, I'll be honest. If not, I'll lie." Or they may say, "If keeping my promise is convenient, I'll keep my promise. If it becomes too costly or uncomfortable, I'll break it." Or, "If being married makes me happy, I'll stay with my wife. If not, I'll leave her."

Conversely, the person of integrity will be faithful to his marriage, or tell the truth, or keep his commitments regardless of how costly, uncomfortable or difficult it may be. In fact, integrity isn't true until it has been tested. It was easy for Daniel to eat only kosher foods in Jerusalem when everyone was doing it, but what about in Babylon when doing so can get you killed? This is the true test of one's character—when it costs.

Integrity Is Not True, Until it Has Been Tested

It's a fact of nature that human beings have the potential to do immoral things if some immediate benefit or payoff is to be gained. A report by University of Utah and Harvard researchers found that individuals who could gain monetarily through unethical behavior were more likely to demonstrate that behavior than those who were not offered a financial gain.[5] Kristin Smith-Crowe, professor of management at the University of Utah, co-authored the study and said, "We certainly found that the love of money is corrupting and just the mere exposure to it makes people do bad things."[6]

It's a precarious reality: Human nature is easily corrupted by the prospect of personal gain. If there is some advantage to receive—whether financial, social or emotional—people are likely to abandon their principles in order to obtain it. This is not to say that money is evil—it's not. What's evil is the affect that money has on us when we love it. At the prospect of getting more and more dollars into our pockets, we often "sell -out" our principles. In the same way, success is not evil. What's evil is the love of success. Too many, in an effort to achieve the next level for status, power or financial gain, have compromised their principles and lowered their standards of integrity. In this context, success can have an insidious effect on human nature.

This is often why God tests our integrity before bringing us to the next level. In fact, those who maintained their integrity during enlargement were also those who went through great hardships on their journey upward. Joseph suffered unimaginable rejection and betrayal prior to his ascension as second in command over Egypt. Moses spent forty years on the backside of the desert before receiving his mantle of prophetic authority. Joshua wandered in the desert with a generation of belligerent complainers before his promotion. David was hunted as a fugitive and traitor on the journey toward his coronation. The list goes on. Each of these endured great tests of character which empowered them with resolute integrity in the place of enlargement.

The Tests Will Come

Psalm 7:9 tells us, "*The righteous God tests the hearts and minds.*" It's a truth often repeated in scripture: See also Jeremiah 17:10 and 20:12, Psalm 11:5 and Proverbs 17:3. God is not impressed by those who proclaim their goodness, He wants us to be confronted with the truth of our integrity—or lack thereof.

Integrity is not true until it has been tested. Anyone can say they are honest when being honest doesn't cost them anything. But true honesty is revealed when telling the truth results in rejection or loss. Anyone can keep their word when fulfilling that commitment is comfortable. But true integrity is revealed when keeping a promise demands sacrifice or extreme inconvenience.

A former church member worked as a bookkeeper on Wall Street. At the end of the financial quarter, he was told by his supervisor to withhold certain details in order to report a profit in one of the departments. He told his boss it was a lie and as a matter of principle, he could not do it. He was fired. But God is faithful, and within thirty days, he had a new job with better compensation and a more favorable work environment.

As a young man I had a promising career in construction. I was offered a lucrative job building a bar where alcohol would be consumed and abused (obviously, it would be a place of drunkenness and revelry). Bound by integrity, I knew it was wrong and I refused. That decision cost me my job and my career in construction. But God is faithful—that decision also opened a door to full-time ministry.

A pastor friend of mine was met after church by a rich parishioner. The man pulled from his pocket a large roll of cash and handed it to the pastor. "This is my tithe," the man said. The pastor replied, "Wait here while I go to the office and get you a receipt." The next Sunday, the same wealthy man approached the pastor again and handed him another wad of cash. "This is my tithe," the man said. The pastor replied, "Wait here while I go to the office and get you a receipt." This ritual went on for several weeks until the pastor noticed one Sunday that the man greeted him, but didn't give him the tithe. Curious, the pastor asked, "Sir, every week you handed me your tithe except today. Is something wrong?" The man replied, "Not at all, I just decided to give my tithe to the office and get my receipt directly from the secretary." Even more curious, the pastor asked, "Why didn't you do that in the first place? Why did you give your tithe to me all these weeks?" The man, with his gaze locked upon the pastor, said, "Because, I was testing you. Before I give my money to this church and bring my family under your ministry, I needed to know if you were a man of integrity. You are." The man wanted to be assured that his tithe would go to God, not to the pastor's pocket.

On your way to the next level, your character will be tested. It's not that God wants to ruin you, He wants to qualify you. 2 Chronicles 16:9 tell us, "*The eyes of the LORD run to and fro throughout the whole earth, to show Himself strong on behalf of those whose heart is loyal to Him.*" God will often bring opportunities to reveal if our integrity can survive the pressures that come at the next level.

God knows that at the next level, the pressure to compromise is always present. There will be people who want access, people who want to use us, and people who simply seek to gratify their own ego by being close to success. Some will even try to corrupt us in order to gain some advantage for themselves.

God knows, at the next level, the opposite sex will present themselves to you; he wants to expose if there are sexual fault lines in your character. He knows, at the next level, more money will flow through your hands. He wants to reveal if there are financial fractures in your integrity. He knows, at the next level, there will be greater admiration from the crowds. He tests our pride to see if our ego is fractured and vulnerable to pride.

The tests will come—because God is preparing us by exposing us. He wants to confront us with the truth about our fractures, to put us on the path to restoration, and prepare us for prolonged success.

The Glory: Enlarging with Humility

If you aspire to the next level, humility is your greatest asset. This is true for two reasons. First, nothing draws the blessing of God into your life like humility. James 4:6 tells us, "*He gives more grace. Therefore, He says: God resists the proud, but gives grace to the humble.*" If you need more grace from God in your life, walk in humility. It's humility that draws God's favor and blessing upon us. James 4:10 says, "*Humble yourselves in the sight of the Lord, and He will lift you up.*" Nothing will take you to the next level like humility.

The second reason why humility is essential is this: The more successful you become, the harder it is to remain humble. It's true: As your influence grows—as God sees your humility and "lifts you up," as you become established, experienced, successful, and respected—the harder it is to stay humble.

This is the subtle danger that resides within going to the next level—it's the tendency to think that because I have been promoted, because I have succeeded, I am more important than those who are "under me."

A classic example of this is found in an Old Testament king name Uzziah.

From Humble Beginnings to Arrogant Success

Uzziah became king at 16 years old. Because he did "what was right in the sight of the Lord," God caused him to prosper. He became exceedingly strong and defeated all his enemies. He conducted great building projects and developed the nation's infrastructure. He raised an army of three hundred thousand warriors and designed technologically advanced weapons. It was all because of God's blessing and his fame spread far and wide.

Unfortunately, as he became successful and famous—as he went to the next level—something happened. 2 Chronicles 26:16 says, "*But when he was strong his heart was lifted up, to his destruction, for he transgressed against the LORD his God by entering the temple of the LORD to burn incense on the altar of incense.*"

When Uzziah went to the next level, his heart changed. He succumbed to a sense of self-importance and pride. He believed himself superior to those around him—even the priests. He reasoned: "I am king. God has favored me above all other men. Thousands of souls bow before me. Why must I defer to some cleric to offer incense for me? I can burn my own incense—I have a 'special' relationship with God and need not submit to a lowly priest."

With this attitude, Uzziah entered the sanctuary and offered incense to God—a blatant violation of mosaic protocol. Immediately, the high priest along with eighty others confronted the king and said, "*It is not for you, Uzziah, to burn incense to the Lord, but for the priests, the sons of Aaron, who are consecrated to burn incense. Get out of the sanctuary, for you have trespassed! You shall have no honor from the Lord God*" (2 Chronicles 26:18). As a result, God judged Uzziah by striking him with leprosy—a sign of God's rejection and public humiliation. King Uzziah was unable to resist the pride that came with his promotion and it ruined him.

Pride is a feeling of exaggerated importance; it's the belief that "I am more important than those around me." Pride is an attitude of self-exaltation that God hates. James 4:6 warns us, "*God resists the proud.*"

When Uzziah went to the "next level," it ruined him. In the beginning, he was a humble man. He sought God and submitted to others. But after he was crowned with authority and achieved success, he started to change. The power he had over others, the control he had over the kingdom, inflated his ego with a perverted sense of importance. This is the danger that is insidious to the success. It's the tendency to think our success makes us more valuable and more important than the people around us. If left unchallenged, this pride can evolve into an attitude of presumption.

Presumption is the assumption that "because I am so important, I should be regarded with a certain level of esteem." In other words, because one has achieved a certain level of success, he expects to receive a certain level of respect.

Uzziah assumed that because he was king and had achieved so much for the kingdom, people would naturally defer to him. He believed that his authority gave him a certain advantage—a special seat that should be automatically respected by everyone around him.

This was the exact attitude that James and John had in Mark 10. They said to Jesus, "*Grant us that we may sit, one on Your right hand and the other on Your left, in Your glory.*" To them, going to the next level was about gaining an advantage for themselves. It was about respect and admiration and being held in high esteem by others. An attitude that Jesus quickly dispelled.

Jesus said to them, "*You know that those who are considered rulers over the Gentiles lord it over them, and their great ones exercise authority over them. Yet it shall not be so among you…whoever desires to become great among you shall be your servant and whoever of you desires to be first shall be slave of all.*"

Jesus confronted this presumption. He made it clear to James and John that any advancement we receive, any success we enjoy, is not for our benefit. It's for the benefit of those around us. If we go to the next level, it's not to enlarge ourselves but to use our position to enlarge others and advance the cause of God.

Unfortunately, if this presumption is not put in check, it will escalate into a sense of entitlement.

Entitlement is a belief that "because of my value, I am 'entitled' to certain privileges and special treatment." It's when people who have achieved certain levels expect to receive certain "perks," benefits or special treatment.

According to Mosaic law, no one burned incense on an altar, except the priests. But Uzziah believed that, because he was king, and such a great man with such importance, that he was entitled to special rights and privileges. It's a sense of entitlement.

There is nothing wrong with receiving honor for your success, or if you're a leader, but never let it become an entitlement. Never allow yourself to believe that because you're the leader, or because of your special accomplishments or special giftings, that you deserve special privileges or special treatment.

Now, leadership should be honored. In the Bible, we are commanded to honor leaders. In fact, 1 Timothy 5:17 tells us, "*Let the elders who rule well be counted worthy of double honor, especially those who labor in the word and doctrine.*" Honoring authority is biblical, and in various cultures, this is done with grace and sincerity. I have been blessed to see people carry the leader's bag, open the leader's door, and give the leaders the best seats. Those are the perks and benefits of leadership. But, as a leader, you must manage the perks with humility.

It's a curious thing that God does. It's as though he wants to provoke our pride, but then commands us to put it in submission. He has created this constant tension in our flesh: Yes, we will be honored, but we must humble ourselves and defer the honor. We are cautioned "not to think of (ourselves) more highly than (we) ought to think," "*giving preference to one another*" (Romans 12:10).

If we go to the next level, there will be perks (benefits). Be we must manage those perks with humility. The perks are a blessing, not an entitlement. Don't let it go to your head. Don't allow your ego to inflate, lest you pick a fight with God.

In fact, sometimes your humility will be tested. In fact, sometimes you will not be honored because God is provoking you—He is pulling on your pride to see what is really in your heart. He wants to know, "Do you really want to be a big shot? Are you trying to become some revered personality or respected authority?" If so, your character is fractured and is unable to support your promotion.

If this sense of entitlement is not defeated, it will putrefy into a feeling of exaltation.

Exaltation is the condition of elevating, promoting and glorifying one's self. It's the tendency to overestimate one's significance, overstep one's boundaries and exceed the limits of one's authority.

Uzziah thought that because he was the great leader—the successful achiever—because he was so smart, so talented and so accomplished, no one could tell him what to do, or what not to do. He went into the sanctuary and offered incense when Mosaic law made it very clear, only the priest was to offer incense. But Uzziah likely imagined, "Who does this lowly priest think he is? I'm the king! I'm smarter, I'm older, I'm more experienced and I don't need him telling me what to do."

It's an act of self-exaltation. It's a demonstration of arrogance. He became haughty and conceited. He had a sense of superiority about himself that was demonstrated in his behavior and attitude. Uzziah was unable to be corrected. He was unteachable, unaccountable, and could not submit. Sadly, leaders start to fall when they can no longer be led, taught, corrected, or criticized.

Qualities of Humility

Uzziah shows us the tragedy of lacking a firm foundation when going to the next level. We fall to pride. It will all be waiting for you at that place of promotion: pride, presumption, entitlement, and exaltation. These are part of the strategy used by those "higher devils at higher levels."

God is looking for humility. However, He's not interested in shallow expressions—He's looking for the real thing.

What is "true humility?" It's that which is demonstrated before our fellow man. In fact, if you're not humble before people, you're not truly humble. Andrew Murray said, "It's not our humility before God that matters, anyone can do that; it's our humility before others that proves if our humility before God is real." Most of us believe that we are humble before God—of course! But true humility is not what you say to God, it's how you act toward others.

True humility is submission. More specifically, it's one's ability to submit to authority. 1 Peter 5:5 says, "... *submit yourselves to your elders. Yes, all of you be submissive to one another, and be clothed with humility, for 'God resists the proud, but gives grace to the humble.'*" King Uzziah rejected correction. He resisted instruction. And, as a result, remained leprous until the day of his death. Regardless of title, level or position, no one is beyond the need of counsel or correction.

To be clear, there is a difference between submission and compliance. Compliance is what happens when we agree with our authority and can easily go along with him or her. If Uzziah agreed with the priest, he would have easily complied. However, it was the priest's resistance and rebuke that tested the sincerity of Uzziah's submission.

Submission is not what happens in times of agreement, it's what happens in times of disagreement. Without disagreement, submission is merely compliance. There is no need to restrain one's impulse or force one's obedience; one needs only to agree with that which he already views favorable. On the contrary, it's the ability to resist that surge of disagreement rising in one's heart that proves his humility. It's that discipline to suppress an impulse of assertion against criticism, advice, or counsel that reveals the presence of real submission.

True humility is teachability. Teachability is the capacity to "*esteem others better than yourself*" (Philippians 2:3) and "*receive instruction*" from them (Proverbs 10:17). Like Uzziah, the proud person believes he has greater gifts, more experience, and better skills than those around him and therefore has no need to listen to or esteem them. But the teachable spirit is willing to admit, "I don't have all the answers."

Most people see themselves as some kind of authority on almost anything. How often we hear, "If I were the leader…, if it was up to me…, if I was the pastor…, this is what I would do." But rather than being wise in his own opinion (Romans 12:16, Proverbs 26:12), the teachable person readily admits, "I need guidance; I don't have all the answers; I need to be led." They are open and appreciative of others' suggestions.

This is a foundational element of going to the next level. Those who do so must never be so arrogant and high-minded that they are beyond correction. While giftedness may take you to the next level, it's your capacity for teachability that will keep you there.

True humility is accountability. Pride resists accountability. The priests told Uzziah he was wrong. Over eighty people told him he was wrong. But that did not matter; it just made him angry. Uzziah held that sensor in his hand and he was going to have HIS WAY.

Accountability implies answerability. It occurs when one party is obliged to report to another party regarding his or her actions and decisions in order to justify them or to suffer consequences in the case of misconduct. It requires checks and balances, transparency and reportability.

The reality is, character is not enough; character must be supported by accountability. No one had more character than King David. God himself described him as "a man after God's own heart." But as a king, no one could tell David what to do. They could suggest, as some did, but he could easily dismiss them. As a result, he fell in sin with Bathsheba and was also deceived by Satan to number Israel.

Accountability is having people around you who have the right and authority to examine your decisions and question your conduct. True accountability is systemic. It's more than a group of friends meeting over coffee—it's built into the structure of the organization, or the DNA of the team. You cannot turn on or off if it becomes too personal or dismiss it if you disagree.

We all need people in our lives to confront us and tell us things that we don't want to hear. Sadly, many people who go to the next level surround themselves with sycophants. They are resistant toward anyone who disagrees or opposes them. However, it's the healthy person, the effective leader, who welcomes contrary opinions and dissenting voices to challenge him and hold him accountable.

The Girls: Enlarging with Purity

Research from the Society for Human Resource Management revealed that 43 percent of HR professionals reported romances in their workplaces.[7] Even more alarming, Wayne Goodall, in his book, *Why Great Men Fall,* revealed that 25 percent of wives and 44 percent of husbands have had extramarital intercourse. Many of their affairs began at "work." Fifty percent of unfaithful wives were involved with someone from work and 62 percent of unfaithful men likewise met their affair partners at work. Indeed sexual promiscuity is a problem in our day, but especially in the workplace.[8]

As you go to the next level, you will undoubtedly confront this growing epidemic in the professional world. Due to proximity, similar interests, time spent together, and physical attractiveness, many people are being sidetracked from their journey to the next level into extramarital affairs.

It's equally true with clergy. Studies reveal that 37 percent of pastors have been involved in inappropriate sexual behavior with someone in their church.[9] Even more alarming is a 15-year study that revealed approximately 10 to 12 percent of ministers have engaged in sexual intercourse with members of their congregations.[10]

How can such respected leaders and ambitious individuals suffer such tragic downfalls? The answer is simple: fractures in the foundation. Good people fall into sexual sin because of the fault lines in their character. In other words, there are places of vulnerability and weakness that cannot resist the pressures of sexual temptation. They have fractures in the foundation—careless professional ethics and relaxed standards of personal purity that have made them susceptible.

If you're going to survive the sexual temptations that are certain to come, you must have a foundation that can bear up under those pressures. The following are several safeguards that can help you avoid the pitfalls of sexual sin. These are more than suggestions, they are ethical mandates for all men and women who wish to protect their integrity as they ascend to the next level.

First, avoid being alone with the opposite sex. Romans 13:14 instructs us to "*Put on the Lord Jesus Christ, and make no provision for* *the flesh, to fulfill its lusts.*" 1 Thessalonians 5:22 further warns us to "*Avoid every appearance of evil.*" This means that leaders must demonstrate due diligence in avoiding situations that present temptation or have the appearance of impropriety, even if intentions are innocent.

Foremost is the danger of being alone with the opposite sex. In a car, having a meeting, sharing a lunch, holding a counseling session—it may seem innocent to you but it has the potential of sending the wrong signal. It says, "I'm interested in you, I don't mind being alone with you," or even worse, "I enjoy being alone with you."

This means men who are spiritual leaders should not have private prayer meetings with women. They shouldn't have one-on-one counseling sessions with women or drive in the car alone with them and never, never, never have lunch or dinner alone with the opposite sex—even in a crowded restaurant.

If I must meet with the opposite sex—I will not meet in a place where we are alone. I always try to meet with others present in the room. If that is not possible or practical, then I will always leave the door open or at least ajar. This sends the message, "We are not really alone" or "I am uncomfortable being alone with you" or more importantly, "I don't want to be alone with you."

In fact, I have instructed my staff on several occasions, "Never leave me alone in the building when there is a woman in my office." And "If you see me in my office with a woman, never pull the door shut, always leave it ajar." As a result, on more than one occasion, someone on my staff has remained late in the office so as to avoid leaving me in a compromising situation.

Some may feel these measures are too extreme or somewhat paranoid. However, I don't believe one can be too careful in the area of sexual purity. Having a casual, relaxed attitude toward the opposite sex can expose good men to subtle and destructive snares.

Second, avoid "Emotional and Spiritual Adultery." In Genesis 2:24 God established the foundation of a healthy marriage: "*Therefore a man shall leave his father and mother and be joined to his wife, and they shall become one flesh.*" The phrase "to be joined" does not just mean to be joined merely in the physical sense; it means that the man and his wife should be joined in every aspect of their being. They are to be joined physically, mentally, emotionally, and spiritually. Unfortunately, there are some men and women who are joining themselves emotionally to someone other than their own spouse. In essence, they are committing "emotional adultery."

Emotional adultery is when one feels more emotionally connected to someone other than his or her own spouse and their emotional needs are being met by someone outside of the marriage. For example, every person has certain "emotional needs." There is "The Need for Significance." A man needs to feel he is special and God has gifted him for a significant purpose that he alone is suited to fulfill. There is also "The Need for Success." Every person needs to believe he or she is achieving greatness and fulfilling the purpose God created him or her for. "The Need for Respect" is similar and speaks to the need we all have to know other people recognize our value and appreciate our significance.

If these needs are being met by anyone other than our own spouse, then you're in an emotionally adulterous affair. If you want to be around some member of the opposite sex more than your own spouse—if you want to talk to her, share personal things with her more than you do with your own wife—you're having an emotional affair. If you're a woman and you look forward to seeing some brother at work and can't wait to be with him, talk to him, share something personal with him, you're committing emotional adultery. Man, do you think about another woman, obsess over her, or daydream about being with her? Do you anticipate seeing her, do you look for her in church or arrange your schedule to see her—if so, you're an emotional adulterer.

As you go to the next level, there will always be a member of the opposite sex who is glad to "build you up," especially if you're a leader. There is something very attractive about leadership (especially in spiritual leadership and the anointing). People who are very needy and emotionally weakened are often drawn to it and enticed by the compassion spiritual leaders demonstrate. They will often say things like, "You are so wise, so gifted. You are such a compassionate and understanding mentor. I love to hear you speak, teach or preach. I'm your biggest fan. I've heard Billy Graham and T. D. Jakes, but you are the best." Take heed leader—don't be naïve. Realize that this is an attempt of the enemy to find fractures in your wall.

If you're committing spiritual or emotional adultery, you must end that relationship immediately! Stop talking to that person. Stop visiting that person. Resolve to never call that person again. Erase her number from your cell phone. If you're on the same team, ask for a transfer immediately. If you're a pastor and she is in your church, you need to break off any contact. Keep your greetings short and sharp and avoid any interaction that encourages emotional or spiritual intimacy between you. Don't worry if that person gets offended and never speaks to you again. For your sake, the sake of your family and sake of the church, that is the best thing that could happen.

Third, don't counsel, coach, or mentor the opposite sex in a way that promotes emotional dependency. Many people today have deep emotional wounds. They may be going through a divorce or suffering neglect in their marriage. They may be reeling from childhood trauma or working through issues of rejection and insecurity. As a result, many of these struggling individuals are very needy. They may lack self-worth, or are looking for affirmation and support. Many are broken-hearted, lonely or afraid. And most are simply looking for a compassionate ear that will listen and validate their pain.

As a compassionate person, you may be inclined to love these suffering souls with empathy and understanding. You realize you have a responsibility to guide them to the Healer who can mend their wounded spirits. However, as we interact with them as coaches and mentors, or pastors, we need to be very cautious. There is a great danger here—a subtle snare—especially when the one coming to us for guidance is of the opposite sex.

The danger occurs when an unhealthy attachment develops. That hurting, needy individual begins seeing you as a special person in their life: a source of empowerment, support and self-worth. As a result, he or she becomes emotionally dependent on you and, if you're not careful, can subconsciously begin to see you as the surrogate parent or spouse they have always longed for.

If that's not bad enough, this dependence can affect you as well. It becomes very gratifying to know that you're so important, so needed, and such a powerful force in someone's life. In fact, many leaders, mentors, and pastors, who themselves are emotionally wounded and insecure, need to be needed. They need to know they are admired, respected, and appreciated. And it's especially gratifying when the one appreciating you is a younger, attractive member of the opposite sex.

It becomes even more gratifying when the leader's emotional needs go unmet in his own marriage. If his wife—or her husband—continually complains and tears him or her down, this may threaten his own self-worth and he may develop a dependency on the counseling relationship. Not because he is receiving counsel, but because he is receiving what he needs emotionally: respect, affirmation, a sense of self-worth—things that he cannot get at home. The result is an emotionally dependent relationship. It's an extremely dangerous fracture. It's very often the beginning of an affair.

There is, however, one rule of leadership that will always cure this fault line: let the sisters counsel the sisters (and the brothers counsel the brothers). Titus 2:3-4 says, "*The older women...(should) admonish the young women.*" The Apostle Paul understood human nature well when he told church leaders to stay away from those young women. "If they need admonition or counsel," the wise apostle wrote, "let the older, godly women take care of it."

A final word. Several years ago the president of a predominate religious seminary issued the following statement following his resignation. "In the final years of my presidency, I yielded to personal temptation by inappropriately engaging in sexual conduct with adult women outside my marriage vows, my pastoral vows, and contrary to Scripture." His ministry ended in shame, embarrassment, and tragedy. He was called to be a vessel for God's glory. Instead, he would be a tool for the enemy to bring reproach on the cause of Christ.

Sadly, we are living in a day when more leaders are falling into sexual sin, financial scandal, and excessive egotism. Their giftedness and competence propelled them to the next level. Success was theirs. Promotion was theirs. But with the success and promotion came pressure and temptation. Because so many lack the foundation—the moral virtues—they are collapsing under the weight of their own success.

Going to the next level is a worthwhile venture. We should all desire to become more effective and influential for the glory of God. However, we must do so with concern for character. Gifting makes a poor foundation for enlargement. Character must precede promotion. Lord, give us more integrity, more humility and more purity.

A FINAL WORD

WHAT GOT YOU HERE, WON'T GET YOU THERE

> **"** ***Every next level of your life will require a different you. What got you here, won't get you there.***

"*Now when they had gone through Phrygia and the region of Galatia, they were forbidden by the Holy Spirit to preach the word in Asia. After they had come to Mysia, they tried to go into Bithynia, but the Spirit did not permit them. So passing by Mysia, they came down to Troas. And a vision appeared to Paul in the night. A man of Macedonia stood and pleaded with him, saying, 'Come over to Macedonia and help us.'*" - Acts 16:6-8

Troas was a Greek city located on the Aegean Sea near the northern tip of Turkey's western coast. It was the chief port of northwest Asia Minor and prospered in Roman times. It was significant in the life of Paul, because he couldn't get to the next level of ministry, until he first went to Troas.

On two consecutive occasions, God prevented Paul's progress in ministry. It was as though he was stuck. He couldn't make the impact he desired to make from the point at which he found himself—he had to get to another destination first. It wasn't until he went to Troas that things began to change for Paul. He would later write in 2 Corinthians 2:12, it was in Troas that "*a door was opened to me by the Lord.*" It was in Troas that revelation came to him and opportunities emerged. It was in Troas that God gave Paul a vision of a man in Macedonia begging him for help.

It was in Troas that Paul would understand what needed to happen to reach the next level.

Many people cannot go the next level until they first go to Troas. It's a place of revelation and redirection—a place where God reveals changes that need to occur before we reach the next level. Your progress to this point in your life has been good. You've been effective at a certain level and succeeded to a certain degree. But what got you here, won't get you to where you want to be. There needs to be a reorientation—a recalibration—if you want to go higher.

As final summation of *Upward: Taking Your Life to the Next Level*, we need to visit Troas. It's a layover in the flight path to your destination. You can't get there without first stopping here and answering five important questions that correct our present course. Think of them as an adjustment in your trajectory. In other words, if you want to arrive at your destination, these changes may need to occur.

What are the habits that hinder your progress?

Habits are your greatest assets or your heaviest burdens. They will push you to success or drive you to disaster. They have propelled men to triumph or buried them in shame. Those that are great, were made great by habit. Those who failed, by habit were made to fail.

We all have them. It could be eating too much, sleeping too long, watching TV late into the night, or posting excessive updates on Facebook. A habit is a repeated behavior that grows stronger each time it's repeated. Unfortunately, those behaviors have the power to determine, not only the quality of our lives today, but the destiny of our lives tomorrow.

Psychologists call it "Future Orientation." It's a concept that describes the trajectory of a person's life based upon their current behaviors. Our attitudes, our lifestyles, are creating a momentum for us that will decide where we end up and how we get there. Some habits orient people toward financial independence. Some habits orient people toward alcoholism or divorce. Other habits can put people on a trajectory toward unemployment, diabetes, loneliness or depression. In fact, it doesn't really matter how well intended one may currently be, or what dreams and aspirations one may have—what matters are habits. They are supreme. They overrule. Habit is king.

You probably know your bad habits; you hardly need someone to point them out to you. What may be less obvious, however, is the impact they are having on you both now and tomorrow. Here's the fact: If you don't get a handle on those habits now, they will hinder you tomorrow. They will become chains around your feet stifling your progress—despite your ambition, intention, sincerity or passion.

So what are your bad habits? Name three of them—right now. What are the worst? What are the three that you know, if left unchecked, will undermine your effectiveness and prevent you from achieving your next level. Overcoming bad habits begins with identifying them—calling them out and labeling them for what they are: enemies to your progress. Once you've identified them, you must then decide if you want to be rid of them. Not everyone is ready to break bad habits. Are you? In fact, this is the real reason why so many never quit smoking, stop drinking, end their complaining, and overcome procrastinating—they really don't want to. But if you're ready, then develop a Holy Spirit empowered strategy and attack that habit like it's an enemy trying to destroy you—because it is.

Some habits are bad, even though they look good. Peter Drucker said, "We spend a lot of time helping leaders learn what to do, we don't spend enough time helping leaders learn what to stop." Francis Chan echoed this when he said, "Our greatest fear should not be of failure, but of succeeding at things in life that don't really matter." Many people are doing things—in fact, they have become proficient in them—but those things are taking them in the wrong direction.

Saul, before he became Paul, was extremely successful. He was great at being a Pharisee. In fact, he was such a successful Pharisee, he was arresting Christians and having them executed. It's the epitome of success in the wrong direction. Stephen Covey wrote, "If the ladder is not leaning against the right wall, every step we take just gets us to the wrong place faster." Saul was climbing a ladder, but every step took him further away from the plan and purpose of God—until God knocked his ladder down.

Is your ladder leaning against the right wall? Before you grind out the lessons of the previous chapters—excellence, mental toughness, diligence, competency, people skills, and moral virtue—first ask yourself, "Where am I going? Am I headed in the right direction?" As you make your ascent to the next level, is your ladder leaning against the right wall? Because if it's not, it's just a matter of time before God will knock it down.

What are the beliefs that limit your growth?

I'm not worried about the big, blatant, obvious lies. I'm not worried about lies such as, "God doesn't love you," or "The Bible isn't true," or

"You're not really saved." Those lies are obvious and easy to detect. The lies I'm concerned about are the ones that aren't obvious; the lies that are couched in just enough truth that they are unlikely to discern. It only takes one drop of cyanide to turn a hundred gallons of water into poison. This is the poison that is the most dangerous—the kind you cannot taste.

Sadly, many people never go to the next level because they are drinking the poison and limiting their growth. The following are three toxic lies that you may be swallowing because they have a twisted resemblance to truth.

I'm not good enough. You're probably right—and you're in good company. Jacob was a cheater, Peter had a temper, David had an affair, Noah was a drunk, Jonah ran away from God, Paul was a murderer, Gideon was insecure, Miriam was a gossiper, Martha was a nervous wreck, Thomas was a doubter, Sarah was impatient, Elijah was depressed, Moses stuttered, Zacchaeus was short, Abraham was old, and Lazarus was dead. God doesn't call the qualified, He qualifies the called. The issue is not our goodness—it's God's grace.

Grace is unmerited favor. We receive it, not because we earned it, but because Christ earned it for us. Colossians 1:12-14 tells us, "*The Father...has qualified us to be partakers of the inheritance of the saints in the light. He has delivered us from the power of darkness and conveyed us into the kingdom of the Son of His love, in whom we have redemption through His blood, the forgiveness of sins.*"

Our qualifications are not based upon "how good we are." We are qualified because of the redemption price paid for us. Redemption means "to buy back" and His blood was the ransom that was paid. We have been purchased out of our slavery and set free in Christ—transferred from the kingdom of darkness into the kingdom of the Son of His love. Jesus paid it all.

The value of a thing is determined by the price one pays to obtain it. Our value to God (which was tarnished and degraded by sin) has been restored by the price Christ paid for us. You're of incredible, eternal value to God, simply by being you. Jesus paid for you and now you're a trophy of His grace—an instrument for His purpose. This means every experience, every struggle, every victory, every failure you bring with you into Christ is a part of your redemption story and has become valuable to the purposes of God.

Alcoholism, bankruptcy, depression, prostitution, incarceration, sickness, disease, mental illness, drug addiction, homelessness—everyone has a fractured past and a painful present. But in Christ, every struggle you've endured is useful to God. He can turn every test into a testimony, every mess into a message, every trial into a triumph and every victim into a victor. Never be ashamed of your story—it's part of your truth and the truth will set others free, by the grace of God.

The people whom God uses the most are the ones who have been shattered and broken the worst, but were put back together by His grace. Many hit bottom, seemed without hope, full of despair and anger and fear. But God stepped into their hopeless prison and redeemed them. He healed them, saved them, delivered them, and gave them a new identity in Christ. It's their story that God uses to illustrate the gospel in modern terms to a new generation. It's their testimony that inspires, uplifts and empowers others to find that same redemption in God that is offered by His grace.

I'm not gifted enough. Of course you're not—that's the point. Henry Blackaby wrote, "Will God ever ask you to do something you're not able to do? The answer is yes—all the time! It must be that way, for God's glory and kingdom. If we function according to our ability alone, we get the glory. If we function according to the power of the Spirit within us, God gets the glory. He wants to reveal Himself to a watching world."

This is why 1 Corinthians 1:24-25 tells us, *"...not many wise according to the flesh, not many mighty, not many noble, are called. But God has chosen the foolish things of the world to put to shame the wise, and God has chosen the weak things of the world to put to shame the things which are mighty.*" He loves weak, incapable people because when they succeed, there can only be one explanation for that success—God did it and God gets the glory!"

When God takes someone to the next level, He doesn't always prepare them first. He doesn't always train them with the right skills and equip them with the right tools so they will have the confidence to fulfill their call. More often, God confronts them with a Goliath, or stops them with a wall of Jericho, or He leads them to a Red Sea, or throws them into a burning fiery furnace and expects them to cry out for help.

Have you ever had the feeling that what you've been called to do is impossible—that there is no way you can achieve it in your own strength? Have you ever stood before a task and thought, "If God doesn't show up—if God doesn't do something miraculous—I am going to fail miserably and be horribly humiliated?" It's called "dependence" and it's exactly where we are supposed to be living. It's what the next level feels like. The feeling that, "I can't do it. This is beyond me. I am in over my head!" is what people who walk by faith usually feel. It's the pathway to the next level and if you're not feeling it, then you're probably not living where God wants you to be living.

It may be true that "you're not gifted enough." It may be true that you lack education or certain skills, but that does not mean that you're disqualified. The next level is not something we achieve on our own strength; it's something we achieve because God made it happen. And it's our sense of dependence on Him that brings the breakthrough. Of course, we must persevere, demonstrate excellence, increase our competencies and be skilled with people. But none of that matters if God's blessing, provision and guidance is not working on our behalf. Do your part—prepare what you can and see how God does the rest.

I sin too much. You mean like Paul? He claimed to be the chief of sinners with a prior reputation for murdering Christians. What about Peter? He denied Christ three times and was later accused of pandering to the Judiazers. We all sin too much. Those who deny this reality are branded by scripture as liars (1 John 1:10).

This issue is not one of moral perfection but moral direction. The work of the Spirit in us is progressive. We have been declared "not guilty" through the sacrifice of Christ; we stand before God justified—positionally holy. But that is just the beginning. God desires that we "*work out (our) own salvation with fear and trembling*" (Philippians 2:12). In other words, He wants to "work out" in our character, the "righteousness" we've been given in Christ. Holiness should become practical and actual in our daily living as we move in the direction of the position we've been given.

It's a journey, not a destination. Yes, we should be moving forward in our progress toward Christlikeness, but we will fall short—a lot. Inevitably, there will be stumbles and falls and failures. The issue, however, is one of context: Are we moving in the right direction or are we sliding back toward the old life? Hebrews 2:1 warns us: "*Therefore we must give the more earnest heed to the things we have heard, lest we drift away.*" The concern is not so much that we have arrived, but that we are moving forward—closer toward Christ, deeper in His Word, submitted to His Spirit and conformed to His image.

This is why I John 2:1-2 gives us this encouragement: "*My little children, these things I write to you, so that you may not sin. And if anyone sins, we have an Advocate with the Father, Jesus Christ the righteous. And He Himself is the propitiation for our sins, and not for ours only but also for the whole world.*" Obviously, we are not given permission to sin. However, it's also obvious that we will sin. The good news is that we need not despair in our failures. We have an advocate with the Father, Jesus Christ the righteous.

This scripture presents the image of a courtroom scene. God the Father is the judge. Before Him stands the guilty sinner—you or me. There is also a prosecutor—the Bible calls him the "Accuser of our brethren, who accused them before our God day and night." This is Satan who fills our minds with condemnation and the fear of being rejected because of our sin. However, standing with us is our Advocate, Jesus Christ the righteous. When the Judge asks, "How do you plead?" the Savior says, "Not guilty—My client pleads the blood—this one is justified and stands before You in My righteousness, free from condemnation!"

Never should we believe we are free to sin, however, if—or when—we do sin, we need not wallow in fear and self-condemnation. We have the confidence that we stand secure in the righteousness of Christ, justified before the throne of God, and free to claim every blessing that is ours through the cross!

Who are the people that are holding you back?

You may have seen the meme circulating on social networks and across the Internet. A man is trapped in a deep hole reaching upward toward another man prostrated on the ground above him. The man, assumed to be his "friend," is reaching down to him, but beyond his grasp. What the man in the hole cannot see, laying conspicuously on the ground next to his "friend" above him, is a ladder hidden from his sight. The caption of the meme reads, "Don't be fooled. Not everyone who appears to help you is actually your friend."

Life is a cycle of seasons. Each season brings new relationships and expands our network of connections. As we transition through seasons, we must discern three types of relationships: bridges, anchors, and chains.

The bridges are those people who connect us to the next level and add propulsion to our purpose and momentum to our movement. These are people who are somehow connected to the next level in our journey and provide certain means to help us up. The means could be in the form of financial resources, mentoring and training, or simply widening our network to others who are also at that next level.

Sometimes these people are with us only for a season. God has strategically connected us to them for the purpose of transition and enlargement. The time may come when the relationship ends. Perhaps they relocate, leave your church, or simply drift away. Don't despair. It's not the end of your life, it's just the end of their part in your life.

Barnabas played a crucial role in Paul's life. He discipled him, encouraged him, helped him to build a network of relationships and then eventually left him. The catalyst for their separation was a disagreement over John-Mark. But it goes deeper. Barnabas was a bridge and he had taken Paul as far as he could. Now that bridge was needed in Mark's life, to take him to the next level. So, Paul's relationship with Barnabas would need to change.

It's important to realize that your bridges are also bridges in other people's lives, not just yours. Don't see them as exclusively your own or become threatened when others connect to them. They serve a special purpose in the Kingdom of God as enablers to those whom God is raising up. Recognize that you have them for a short time—that season may soon end and so may your connection to them.

Recognize that bridges are not necessarily interested in you. In fact, they are usually more interested in what you *do*. In other words, they share with you a common cause, a common mission. They will team up with you to help fight your cause because it's also their cause. But when the mission is accomplished, they move on. They are like scaffolding—once the building is done, they are gone. But they are necessary to your cause and necessary to your growth. Just don't be upset that they are not passionate about you personally.

The important thing to remember is this: Don't burn the bridges. If you try to hold onto someone that God is moving out of your life, the relationship will sour. If they are not meant to be with you, don't try to hold onto them. You will be getting in God's way and God will have to burn the bridge to free it from your grip.

This is why so many relationships have become toxic and so many disqualify themselves for the next level before they even get there. When people leave, or disconnect, or no longer show an interest in them, they become personally offended. They internalize it as a form of rejection and believe their former friend sees them as somehow deficient or inadequate and therefore rejects them. Hardly ever is this the case. More likely, it's a matter of seasons. Some people will be with us for a short time, to propel us forward, and then they are gone.

By contrast, the anchors never leave. **The anchors are those relationships who remain vital to our life purpose and keep us connected to vital truths regardless of seasons.** These relationships stay with us through each level we as we progress. They are anchors. They remain constant and steadfast and are crucial to our growth, health, stability and security. The anchors keep you grounded, humble and healthy no matter how high you may climb.

Moses had Joshua, David had Abishai, and Esther had Mordecai.

The anchors are interested in you and care about you—not what you can do for them, and not how they benefit from having you. God has raised them up to support and sustain you. The anchors are not looking for you to feed them or empower them, or elevate them; they want to feed you, empower you, and elevate you.

Sometimes, they will hurt you—but only because you need to be hurt. Sometimes they will let you down—but only because you're climbing the wrong ladder. Sometimes, they will oppose you—but only because they know it's for your own good. Through it all, they will love you, pray for you, defend you and stand with you without any hope of recognition or reward. They are motivated simply by a love for you that has been given to them by God.

Thank God for the anchors. If you're hurting, they are there. If you fail, they are there. If you succeed, they are there. If you become famous and successful beyond your wildest dreams, they are there—keeping you grounded to reality. The anchors are often family members or spouses. They can be parents or early mentors that have never left. Pastors are often anchors, as are teachers or professors who provided essential education. Sometimes the anchors are simply friends who know us best—our blemishes, bruises, faults and failures—but still love us, accept us and cheer us on. Thank God for the anchors.

And then, there are the chains. **The chains are relationships that developed during a certain season of our life, but must be let go of in order to progress.** They hinder our growth. They hold us back. They are chains that put limits on our advancement. Remember the meme: "Don't be fooled. Not everyone who appears to help you is actually your friend." As you transition through the seasons of life, you will need to discern which people are preventing you from evolving and respond to them accordingly.

Some chains don't realize they are chains. I once had an employee who refused to upgrade her skills. Because of her limited abilities and lack of competence, she became a drag on our team. Her employment was absorbing limited resources and prevented us from acquiring the necessary skills to go to the next level. In a former season, she was a bridge—she had helped us to go to a new level. Unfortunately, she believed herself to be irreplaceable, never trained up, and became a chain. There was only one choice. Her position was eliminated and a new one was created which required higher skill sets. Once those chains were removed, the office began to flourish, new goals were set and reached, and a new season of growth was achieved.

For you, it could be an underachieving employee, a friend who drinks too much, a mentor you've outgrown or a coworker who complains and undermines the team. At one point, they may have been a bridge, someone that encouraged you, inspired and challenged you to go higher and try new things. But, now you realize their beliefs and behaviors are small-minded and immature. You've outgrown those attitudes, and in order to go to the next level, you must abandon them.

It may be time to move on. Cut the cord. If you want to change, if you want to go higher, you must let go of those things that hold you back. What got you here, can't get you there. You can try to be nice and explain the change. You can ask them to come along and be supportive. But the bottom line is this: You cannot change what you're unwilling to confront.

Some chains are intentionally chains—and intentionally want to hold you back. Because of their own insecurities, they see your progression as a threat. They mistakenly perceive how your growth may negatively impact them or reflect upon their own inferior complex, so they sabotage your advance.

Sadly, this is often the case and it explains why people can be chains: They are mostly interested in you because of what you can do for them. They care about you because they need you—because of how you make them feel or how you make them better. Hardly ever will this person show an interest in what you need or how they can improve you—the relationship is very one sided, focused mainly on their needs and what they expect from you. In fact, if you show any promise of going to the next level, the chains often become threatened. Their fear of losing you causes them to somehow oppose, prevent, or hinder you from your advance.

In these relationships, you will have to make a choice. Will you be an enabler or will you be a bridge? Enablers promote weakness and dependency. Instead of confronting bad behavior, they provide an environment that perpetuates the behavior. It's a wife that conceals her husband's abuse rather than exposing it. It's a boss that tolerates an employee's poor work product rather than demanding improvement. It's a parent who provides support for a child's addiction rather than forcing an intervention. By contrast, bridges act as points of transition where bad behavior is either forced to change or left behind. Become a bridge. Don't enable and pander to those who are sabotaging your advance. Confront their behavior or leave them behind. But don't be a victim to their toxic mindset.

The truth is, no one is holding you back—that makes you sound like a powerless victim. The only way someone can "hold you back" is by giving him or her the power to do so. Eleanor Roosevelt said, "No one can make you feel inferior without your consent." When we say that someone is holding us back, it's because we gave them the power to do so.

If you've ever been to a zoo, perhaps you seen the huge elephants who are confined merely by a small rope tied to their leg. No massive chains, no cages. At any time, those gigantic beasts could easily break the rope, but for some reason, they don't.

The reason for their confinement is at a young age, trainers use these same ropes to tie them and, at that age, it's enough to hold them back. As they grow up, they are conditioned to believe they cannot break away—and never try to do so. It's amazing. These elephants are massive and powerful, yet they allow their own potential to be limited because they believe the presence of the rope on their leg means they cannot get free.

Sometimes, relationships can be like ropes around our feet. Because of our history with someone—perhaps they were a bridge that mentored us and brought us to the next level—we believe we "need" them and dare not wander beyond their guidance or control. In a sense, they have become a hindrance in your life that limits you own personal potential. You have tied yourself to their potential and allowed them to define your purpose only as it relates their success.

Obviously, there will be those lifetime anchors to whom God will connect us: these ties should be preserved. But there will be those who are meant only for a season and when that season ends, it's time to cut the rope.

What are the failures you need to forget?

The enemy capitalizes on our failures. He is the "Accuser of the Brethren." He specializes in bringing us into condemnation and feeling such overpowering shame that we prevent ourselves from being used by God. As a pastor, I have seen this as a primary means that the devil uses to stop people from going to the next level. As soon as God starts using them, making them effective and providing opportunities, the shame they feel causes them to withdraw, isolate, and even sabotage the good things God is doing in their lives.

Paul said, "*Forgetting those things which are behind, I reach forward to those things which are ahead.*" And he had much to forget. In fact, in Acts 8:3 it says, "*...he made havoc of the church, entering every house, and dragging off men and women, committing them to prison.*" Undoubtedly, he carried a sense of regret and shame for his past sins and considered himself the "*chief of sinners*" (1 Timothy 1:15).

As terrible as his past sins were, it provides a powerful example for us. If God can take Saul, a murderer and persecutor of the church, and transform him into the "Apostle to the Gentiles," using him to write nearly half the New Testament, God can use you and me. The problem, however, is not with God's ability to forgive and repurpose our lives, it's in our ability to forgive and repurpose ourselves.

If you're going to go the next level, you must let go of your shame. When Jesus hung on that cross, he bore your sins. He took the punishment and bore the wrath of God in your place. Micah 7:19 tells us, "*He has cast all our sins into the depths of the sea—the sea of forgetfulness—never to be seen or heard from again.*" Ephesians 1:6 says, "*He made us accepted in the Beloved.*" Through the blood of Christ, we are forgiven, cleansed, and restored as sons and daughters of God. He accepts us just as we are. Stop trying to earn your acceptance with God by doing good deeds and acting spiritual. Accept your acceptance with God.

You may be reading this book with a secret sense of condemnation. Many people are grieved over the idea of going to the next level because they feel so unworthy. The guilt over sins they've committed and people they've wounded has convinced them that they should have no right to expect should favor and goodness from God.

But the devil is a liar. The blood of Jesus has cleansed you just as the Apostle Paul was cleansed. Accept your acceptance, forget your failures, and "press toward the goal for the prize of the upward call of God in Christ Jesus."

What are the victories you need to expect?

Many people are intimidated by the next level because it often involves a challenge. In fact, the prospect of battle is why so many never get there. They are simply afraid of the risk involved, and what they might lose in the event of failure.

Truly, there may be risk, but it's one's willingness to overcome that risk and achieve a victory that distinguishes him or her for the next level. We see it in Moses and the Red Sea, David's confrontation with Goliath, Joshua and the walls of Jericho, Gideon's battle with the Midianites, and Daniel's visit to the lion's den. It's a person's ability to face the challenge and believe God for victory against insurmountable odds that demonstrates his or her quality.

Your next level will not "just happen." It will be preceded by a challenge—a risk. Some dilemma, some crisis or tragedy, will present itself and you will have an opportunity to step up and take action. Will there be a danger? Yes, absolutely. Will it be frightening and intimidating? Without a doubt. But it's the one who faces their fear and pushes through it that is distinguished. Expect victory, have faith, demonstrate courage—not based upon your ability, but based upon a confidence in God.

> *"Not that I have already attained, or am already perfected; but I press on, that I may lay hold of that for which Christ Jesus has also laid hold of me. Brethren, I do not count myself to have apprehended; but one thing I do, forgetting those things which are behind and reaching forward to those things which are ahead, I press toward the goal for the prize of the upward call of God in Christ Jesus."* - Philippians 3:12-14

ENDNOTES

Chapter One

1. Retold from *What a Day This Can Be*, John Catoir, ed., Director of the Christophers (New York: The Christophers)
2. C.S. Lewis. 1959. "Screwtape proposes a toast," in *The Screwtape Letters*. San Francisco: Harper Collins, reprint 2001, Page 201
3. See http://www.merriam-webster.com/dictionary/discipline; accessed February 2016
4. See https://www.goodreads.com/quotes/310930-the-less-you-associate-with-some-people-the-more-your; accessed February 2016
5. See http://time.com/money/3678511/ebay-amex-baker-hughes-layoffs; accessed February 2016
6. See http://www.thestreet.com/story/13437444/1/apple-aapl-stock-tumbles-on-expected-sales-decline-jim-cramer-set-to-outperform.html; accessed February 2016
7. See http://www.beckersasc.com/asc-turnarounds-ideas-to-improve-performance/5-common-employee-disciplinary-issues-at-ascs-how-to-overcome-them.html; accessed February 2016
8. Samuel R. Chand. 2015. *Leadership Pain.* Nashville: Thomas Nelson, Page 81
9. Research conducted by Angus Reid on behalf of RSM Richter; see http://www.rsmrichter.com/pressrelease.aspx?ID=141; Accessed November 2009
10. See video: The Science of Pornography Addiction - http://www.youtube.com/watch?v=1Ya67aLaaCc; accessed March 2016
11. Wayne Goodall. 2005. *Why Great Men Fall.* Green Forest, Arizona: New Leaf Press, Page 57

Chapter Two

1. See http://www.lifewithoutlimbs.org/about-nick/bio; accessed December 2015
2. See http://seanstephenson.com; accessed December 2015
3. See http://www.christianpost.com/news/survey-reasons-why-people-leave-the-church-22882; accessed December 2015
4. Jim Collins. 2001. *Good to Great.* New York, NY: HarperCollins, Page 83
5. Jones, G., Hanton, S., & Connaughton, D. 2002. *What Is This Thing Called Mental Toughness? An Investigation of Elite Sport Performers. Journal of Applied Sport Psychology,* 14(3), Page 209
6. Dr. Caroline Leaf. 2013, Page 32, *How to Switch on Your Brain.* Grand Rapids, MI.: Harper Books, Page 32
7. Outnumbered, Fox News Channel, February 8, 2016
8. John Piper. 2003. *Desiring God.* Sisters, Oregon: Multnomah, Page 302
9. Eric Greitens. 2015. *Resilience*. Boston: Houghton Mifflin Harcourt, Page 16

Chapter Three

1. See *The Road to Character,* David Brooks at www.youtube.com; accessed December 2015
2. See https://www.psychologytoday.com/basics/procrastination; accessed January 2016

Chapter Four

1. Sylvia Ann Hewlett, 2014. *Executive Presence.* New York: HarperCollins,

Page 6
2. Richard Bandler, 1990. *Frogs into Princes: Neuro Linguistic Programming.* Eden Grove Publishers
3. Sylvia Ann Hewlett, 2014. *Executive Presence.* New York: HarperCollins, Page7
4. Ibid, Page 8

Chapter Five

1. See http://millennialbranding.com/2014/05/multi-generational-job-search-study-2014; accessed March 2016
2. Bill Hybels. 2008. *Axiom*. Grand Rapids, MI: Zondervan, Page 75
3. Dale Carnegie, 1936 (revised 1982). *How to Win Friends and Influence People.* New York: Pocket Books, Page 14
4. Ibid, Page 67
5. Oracle White Paper: A Global Perspective, The International Journal for Listening, Vol. 14, UCLA study, Dr. Albert Mehrabian; Harvard Business Review, BusinessWeek
6. Ibid
7. John Bevere. 1994. *The Bait of Satan.* Orlando, FL: Creation House, Page 13
8. Ibid, Page 15

Chapter Six

1. John Maxwell. 2000. *The 21 Most Powerful Minutes in a Leader's Day.* Nashville: Thomas Nelson.
2. J. Robert Clinton. 1990. *Listen Up Leaders: Forewarned is Forearmed.* Barnabas Publishers, Page 6
3. Ibid, Page 3
4. See Richard J. Krejcir, *"Statistics on Pastors,"* http://www.intothyword.org/apps/article /default.asp?articleid=36562; accessed March 2016
5. Kouchaki, M., Smith-Crowe, K., Brief, A. P., & Sousa, C. 2013. *Seeing green: Mere exposure to money triggers a business decision frame and unethical outcomes. Organizational Behavior and Human Decision Processes*
6. See http://www.cnbc.com/id/100810791; accessed March 2016
7. See http://www.businessnewsdaily.com/5921-flirting-with-trouble-office-romances-can-prove-costly.html#sthash.kakKJqaF.dpuf; accessed March 2016
8. Wayne Goodall. 2005. *Why Great Men Fall.* New Leaf Press, Green Forest, Arizona, Page 12 (quoting Shirley Glass, "Not Just Friends")
9. H. B. London, Jr., and Neil B. Wiseman. 1993. *Pastors at Risk*, Wheaton: Victor, Page 22
10. Joe E. Trull and James E. Carter. 1993. *Ministerial Ethics: Being a Good Minister in a Not-So-Good World.* Nashville: Broadman and Holman, Page 81

About the Author

Gregg Johnson is Lead Pastor of The Mission Church where he has served for over twenty-five years. Known for its emphasis on foreign missions, community outreach, leadership development and discipleship programs, The Mission Church is a vibrant, growing church making an impact for Jesus Christ both locally and internationally.

Ordained with the Assemblies of God, Pastor Gregg served for over nine years as Assemblies of God New York Ministry Network Presbyter for the Hudson Valley Section. Currently, he serves as Executive Presbyter for the Eastern Region of the AGNY Ministry Network. In these capacities, he has acted as ministry coach and consultant to various churches, pastors and leadership teams in the Eastern Region of New York State.

Rev. Gregg Johnson is also founder and keynote speaker of Global Leadership Training, providing ministry coaching, study materials and leadership training conferences to church, civic and corporate leaders throughout East and West Africa, India, Cuba, Canada, and the United States. Frequently, these conferences are endorsed and attended by national and local government authorities, corporate executives and religious denominational leaders.

Pastor Gregg has authored seven books on leadership and personal development including, *Upward: Taking Your Life to the Next Level, How the Mighty Have Fallen, The Trust of Leadership, The Character of Leadership, Raising the Standard of Leadership, Ethics for Church Leaders*, and *Crisis, Conflict and Change*. He is founder and publisher of Leadership Teaching Magazine and regularly publishes an online blog that addresses important topics on leadership, ministry and personal growth targeting leaders in developing countries around the world.

Pastor Gregg and his wife Laura live in New York, have raised five children and have two grandchildren.

www.GreggTJohnson.com

www.GlobalLeadershipTraining.org

www.LeadershipTeachingMagazine.com

www.MissionChurch.com

Other Leadership Publications
by Gregg T. Johnson

The Character of Leadership

Raising the Standard of Leadership

Ethics for Church Leaders

Crises, Conflict and Change

How the Mighty Have Fallen

The Trust of Leadership

Upward! Taking Your Life to the Next Level

Leadership Teaching Magazine
A 24-page online magazine which addresses important topics on leadership and ministry. Download for free at www.LeadershipTeachingMagazine.com.

To order books contact:

The Mission Church
4101 Rt. 52
Holmes, NY 12531
info@missionchurch.com
(845) 878-3380

Discounts available for bulk orders

To view products online or check out more articles on leadership, go to:
www.GreggTJohnson.com